PERSPECTIVE AND GUIDANCE
FOR A TIME OF DEEP DISCORD

Also by Charles Johnston:

The Creative Imperative: Human Growth and Planetary Evolution

Necessary Wisdom: Meeting the Challenge of a New Cultural Maturity

Pattern and Reality: A Brief Introduction to Creative Systems Theory

The Power of Diversity: An Introduction to the Creative Systems Personality Typology

An Evolutionary History of Music: Introducing Creative Systems Theory Through the Language of Sound (DVD)

Quick and Dirty Answers to the Biggest of Questions: Creative Systems Theory Explains What It Is All About (Really)

Cultural Maturity: A Guidebook for the Future

Hope and the Future: Confronting Today's Crisis of Purpose

On the Evolution of Intimacy: A Brief Exploration into the Past, Present, and Future of Gender and Love

Rethinking How We Think: Integrative Meta-Perspective and the Cognitive "Growing Up" on Which Our Future Depends

Creative Systems Theory: A Comprehensive Theory of Purpose, Change, and Interrelationship in Human Systems (with Particular Pertinence to Understanding the Times We Live in and the Tasks Ahead for the Species)

Online:

Author/professional page: www.CharlesJohnstonMD.com
The Institute for Creative Development: www.CreativeSystems.org
Creative Systems Theory: www.CSTHome.org
Cultural Maturity: www.CulturalMaturity.org
The Creative Systems Personality Typology: www.CSPTHome.org
An Evolutionary History of Music: www.Evolmusic.org
Cultural Maturity: A Blog for the Future: www.CulturalMaturityBlog.net
Looking to the Future podcast: www.LookingtotheFuture.net

PERSPECTIVE AND GUIDANCE FOR A TIME OF DEEP DISCORD

Why We See Such Extreme Social and Political Polarization—and What We Can Do About It

CHARLES M. JOHNSTON, MD

The Institute for Creative Development (ICD) Press

Seattle, Washington

Publisher's Cataloging-In-Publication Data
(Prepared by The Donohue Group, Inc.)

Names: Johnston, Charles M., author.
Title: Perspective and guidance for a time of deep discord : why we see such
    extreme social and political polarization--and what we can do about it /
    Charles M. Johnston, MD.
Description: Seattle, Washington : The Institute for Creative Development
    (ICD) Press, [2021] | Include bibliographical references and index.
Identifiers: ISBN 9781734243116 (print) | ISBN 9781734243123 (ebook)
Subjects: LCSH: Polarization (Social sciences)--History--21st century. | Right
    and left (Political science)--History--21st century. | Social problems--
    History--21st century. | Interpersonal communication--History--21st
    century. | Social sciences--Philosophy.
Classification: LCC HN90.P57 J64 2021 (print) | LCC HN90.P57 (ebook) |
    DDC 306.09--dc23

The Institute for Creative Development (ICD) Press, Seattle, Washington

Cover design by Wilson Piechazek

Author photo by Brad Kevelin

ISBN: 9781734243116
Library of Congress Control Number: 2020915181   First printing 2021

PERSPECTIVE AND GUIDANCE
FOR A TIME OF DEEP DISCORD

Discord and Discontent

In the early weeks of the coronavirus pandemic, a client asked me whether I thought conversations about the virus would in time become polarized. I've written extensively about how extreme polarization is the fate of most issues today even if the concern initially has no obvious sides. I responded that I suspected we would at first find almost the opposite. People tend to do a remarkably good job of pulling together in the face of real crisis. But I also predicted that we would see significant polarization eventually, given this general tendency combined with the huge stresses that dealing with the pandemic would create. The media's need for sensationalized content in the face of something as tedious and drawn out as a pandemic adds to this likelihood. I warned in articles that I wrote at the time that we should be particularly careful about the creation of false dichotomies between health concerns and economic worries. But I also observed that it was hard to predict just what animosities and allegiances would arise and where battle lines would get drawn. I could not have guessed that we would eventually find polarization over whether a person should wear a face mask. The pandemic could have united us, but our responses to it ended up dividing us even further.

As a cultural psychiatrist and futurist, I have worked over the course of my life to bring big-picture perspective to critical human questions. That has involved decades leading the Institute for Creative Development, a think tank and center for advanced training in Seattle, and writing numerous books and articles on the future and what it asks of us. It has also involved developing conceptual frameworks that can help us make sense of both the possibilities and the dangers that our times present. In particular, it has involved the development of Creative Systems Theory. The theory includes the concept of Cultural Maturity,[1] the idea that our times are demanding—and beginning to make possible—an essential "growing up" as a species.[2]

This book takes as its starting point a danger that has come to concern me greatly of late—one that leaves us far from the greater maturity of understanding my work has been about. With issues of every sort, people today are dividing almost immediately into polar camps. Often with particular issues it is not at all clear in advance that there is any reason for conflict. All we know is that division will happen eventually and will result in absolutist advocacy from both sides. Conflict between ideological factions today has become so pronounced that real conversation about a great many topics has become largely impossible. Many others besides myself who attempt to make sense of the human condition have pointed toward the dangers this circumstance presents. Extreme polarization is setting neighbor against neighbor, creating distraction that gets in the way of addressing essential questions, and often very directly putting us at risk. Over the last couple of decades, we've seen such reactive polarization become ever more pronounced and people's voices becoming ever more shrill.

---

[1]   I will capitalize formal Creative Systems Theory terms throughout the book.

[2]   The most complete explication of Creative Systems Theory (CST) can be found in my book *Creative Systems Theory: A Comprehensive Theory of Purpose, Change, and Interrelationship in Human Systems* (ICD press, 2021). For the most detailed examination of the concept of Cultural Maturity, see *Cultural Maturity: A Guidebook for the Future* (ICD Press, 2015).

Here I will briefly address why we may be witnessing what we do. Depending on the explanation, the implications could be very different. Then, with the larger portion of the book, I will turn to the question of just what getting beyond this dangerous and ultimately untenable circumstance will require of us. The solution I will put forward is different from what many people might expect. It is not just moderation. It is also different from being willing to listen and find compromise— although any of these things might be a step forward. Rather, it has to do with needed new steps in how we understand and lead, steps that will be required if we are to effectively address most any of the important questions ahead for us as a species.

A simple lesson will provide the architecture for the book: In times past, when we encountered polarized positions and partisan advocacy, our task was obvious and unquestioned. We assumed that there were only two options and that our job was to figure out which one was right and fight for it. As we look to the future, polarization has very different implications. It alerts us to the fact that we have yet to ask the hard questions that ultimately need to be addressed. When we succeed at asking the larger questions, we see that there have always been more than just two sides. We also see that while each traditional side may hold a piece of the truth, neither side by itself, nor just some averaging of positions, can get us where we need to go. Moving forward effectively will require bringing greater maturity, and more encompassing perspective, to how we make sense of our worlds and how we make choices.

Acknowledging the Consequences and the Tasks Ahead

The consequences of social and political polarization have become increasingly significant—at multiple levels. At a personal level, partisan animosities make it difficult simply for people to get along. Differences are dividing families and damaging friendships. They also add in critical ways to the sense of cynicism and hopelessness that is increasingly prevalent in our time. Nelson Mandela observed that "having a grievance or resentment is like drinking poison and hoping it will kill the enemy." The fact of intractably incompatible beliefs is a further contributor to what Creative Systems Theory refers to as our modern Crisis of Purpose. Many people today have lost a basic sense of hope and direction in their lives.[3]

Partisan animosities are also significant because of the effect they have on the functioning of institutions. This is most obvious with government. Today in the U.S., partisan pettiness is making it nearly impossible to pass even the simplest of legislation. It could well be that if we can't get beyond current simple-answer reactive thinking, the democratic experiment that we've fought so hard for over the last 250 years might not weather our shortsightedness.

And while the claim might sound extreme, we may in fact be putting our human survival at risk. We confront multiple dangers today that could well be the end of us. The top five on my list (in no particular order): the risk of nuclear annihilation, climate change and its consequences, how the growing gap between the world's haves and have-nots risks global economic destabilization, misuse of emerging technologies, and the growing potential for widespread disease. It is clear that effectively confronting any of the first four will require that we get beyond seeing the world in polarized, us-versus-them terms. I had not previously framed addressing the risks of worldwide disease in this way, but the 2020 pandemic has made it obvious that there, too, failing to bring more encompassing perspective to bear could be our undoing.

I will give special attention here to a more basic danger. Extreme social and political polarization distracts us from the overarching task on which our future ultimately depends. In my writing through the

---

[3]   In my book *Hope and the Future: Confronting Today's Crisis of Purpose* (ICD Press, 2018), I tie this larger crisis to today's increasing rates of suicide,

years, I've come back repeatedly to the recognition that addressing any of the most important questions ahead for the species will require that we think in more mature and complete—more systemic—ways. It will demand approaches to making decisions that better engage the whole of who we are, and with this, the full nuance and complexity of what we wish to make sense of. Fights between competing ideologies not only get in the way of finding needed more encompassing solutions, they make it very hard to recognize the questions that we need to confront. And, more generally, they get in the way of developing the capacities and new ways of understanding needed if we are to act constructively and move forward effectively.

A person could legitimately argue that this book's title is misleading. It might seem to imply that there are simple remedies for absurdities that too often today monopolize social discourse. I will argue that there are remedies—in fact, they are precisely what this book is about. But these are not remedies of the simple, do-this-then-do-that sort. And they will not make everyone happy. Certainly these are not remedies in the sense of tricks to convince those who we might not agree with that we are right—which writings that claim to reconcile differences on close examination too often prove to be. They are also not the kinds of solutions commonly put forward by people committed to fairness and mutual understanding. Being willing to meet others halfway has an important place, but rarely does it in itself produce the kind of change that will ultimately be necessary. The remedies that I will suggest can be thought of as ultimately simple, but they are not easy. They require revisiting how we understand both ourselves and the world around us.

It could even be argued that this book isn't really about polarization—even extreme polarization. When I hear polarized opinions, I start with the assumption that I am witnessing left and right hands of a

---

depression, and addiction.

larger systemic picture. And I know that simply adding aspects together doesn't produce the needed more systemic result. Thus I don't find the content of polarized opinions very interesting. They tend to be tediously predictable, and rarely are they helpful as far as solutions.

In the chapters ahead, we will look at how our times challenge us to confront questions that are new and often deeply demanding in what they ask of us. We will also examine how getting beyond the polarized assumptions of times past—and certainly the kind of extreme polarized and polarizing thought that we encounter today—will be essential to going forward. And we will take beginning steps toward understanding the more encompassing and complete kinds of thinking and decision-making that will be necessary if we are to effectively make our way.

A Challenge Equally for the Right and the Left

A recognition that has only in recent years become fully clear to me warrants attention before we dive into the book's more specific reflections. Fifteen years ago, if you asked me whether the political right or the political left was being more regressive and absurd in its claims, the answer would be obvious. The Right had become consumed by an increasingly populist worldview that made government itself the problem. Its actions undermined not just effective governance, but any possibility of constructive conversation. I am always careful of false equivalences, but today I find the Left often seeming as absurd and regressive in its ideological assertions, and often just as much an obstacle to mature understanding and effective policy. Extreme populism on the Left can end up being little different than the more familiar fanatical populism of the Right, and when it does, it gets us no closer to the truth.

Why is this observation important? Most obviously it is important so that we don't get caught in thinking that the task is only to decide which side in a polarized debate is correct. I will propose that in fact the Right and the Left in our time, and not just in their more extreme forms, but more basically, each stop fundamentally short of what is needed.

The observation is also important because the larger portion of people who will choose to read this book will likely share more liberal leanings, or at least have had liberal leanings in times past. It would be nice if those on the Right would have equal interest, but that will be unusual. Liberals tend to be more interested in change and the future (this is why they call themselves progressives), even if their ideas about what such change should entail often leave out essential pieces of what needs to be considered.

It is important, too, if we are to effectively parse out information in today's world of conflicting messages, info glut, and outright fake news. Not too long ago, we at least had trusted agents in the sense of people committed to "balanced" reporting—think Walter Cronkite or Edward R. Murrow. The kind of perspective that I will propose is essential to going forward is about more than balance in this sense. But increasingly even balanced reporting in a traditional sense is a rare luxury. We've come to have a media of the Right and a media of the Left. And while the media of the Right may be most obviously ideological and absurd in its assertions, the media of the Left has often today become just as predictable (and here I include the best of liberal media— for example, the *New York Times* and public radio and television[4]). And precisely because of its identification with being good and fair, media on the Left can be particularly oblivious to its ideological blindnesses.

It will also likely be people who come out of more liberal traditions who will be most called on to provide leadership going forward. I come

---

4   Over a five-year period twenty years back, I led an internal think tank within Seattle's public television station that attempted to address how public media could provide the most powerful leadership in decades ahead. I wish I could say that more of that vision had been realized.

back to the fact that liberals tend simply to be more interested in the future. The conservative tendency to try to retain what has value can ultimately contribute just as much. But passion from the Left is often what puts change in motion. For this reason, too, the kind of perspective this book provides could have particular importance for people of more liberal bent. This reason takes on particular urgency with the recognition that the Left today is often proving just as effective as the Right in undermining real change.

I will sometimes excerpt from writing I've done previously to help put key points in context. I wrote the following blog post in the last few months of Donald Trump's presidency. It captures the depth of my concerns.

A Very Disturbing and Dangerous Situation—Political Polarization and Populism Run Amok

I was awakened in the middle of the night this week with a disturbing recognition. We are seeing the rise of a regressive left-wing populism that is not that different from the right-wing populism that put our current U.S. president in power.

It is a reality that troubles me in terms of humanity's general well-being. None of the really important questions of our time can be addressed from the positions of either extreme. And certainly the last thing we need is more polarized drama and distraction in times that are demanding enough.

This reality also troubles me in a more personal sense. My life's work has involved training leaders in the more mature and systemic kind of thinking needed to address most any of the really important questions ahead for the species. In the present context, when it might seem that my contribution could not be more important, I find myself at an impasse. I can't come close to saying what ultimately needs to be said about most any issue today without violating political correctnesses of either the Right or the Left, and commonly both at once. And these are not quibbles about details. In making the most obvious elephant-in-the-room assertions, I am challenging beliefs that each side regards not just as true, absolutely, but sacred.

On waking, I found myself asking a question that I never thought I would consider, and that would not occur to me in a waking state. In Seattle, where I live, there is a person on the city council who identifies as a socialist and consistently says things that are quite beyond comprehension, and that are as inflammatory as anything our current president would say. I consider our current president to be not just the worst in U.S. history, but someone who presents particular dangers for our time. I found myself asking that if our city council person were to run against him, who I would vote for. In fact, that situation would never present itself and I wouldn't vote for either of them if it did. But it leaves the question of who would be the most dangerous. His dangers have less to do with ideology than his basic mental health. The councilwoman is an absolutist, unswerving, simple-answer ideologue.

To be clear, I am not just complaining about extremism, which has always been a problem. Middle-of-the-road thinking gets us no closer. As a start, I'm talking about leaders claiming to present "big" ideas when in fact they are failing to ask the hard questions. And of particular concern, I'm talking about how large a percentage of people on both the Right and the Left are today finding comfort in becoming hoards of the like-minded—all too ready to collude in ignoring the complexities of what our times ask of us.

I've written extensively about how our future well-being will require a sophistication of understanding that before now would not have been an option. Instead, we are seeing regressive thinking across the board. Given the magnitude of the challenges we face, if we are not willing to open our eyes, we could find ourselves in increasing peril.

There is a good reason why I might wake up feeling disturbed. Sometimes issues that come with middle-of-the-night awakenings temper considerably with the light of day. I am now awake, and I feel even more concerned.[5]

An observation implied in this piece puts an exclamation point on the particular significance of our time and the importance of finding some way forward. It is not just that we see increasing conflict between the positions of the Right and the Left; we find assertions from both the Right and the Left that are really quite nonsensical—indeed, rather crazy. In having conversations with the best of thinkers, more and more often I encounter outright bewilderment at what we witness today and the use of words like "lunacy" in their desperate attempts to make sense of it. And I find the people who have the maturity to engage questions with the needed complexity all too often walking on eggshells to avoid the endless ideological land mines.

This book will come at today's circumstances and what our future asks of us from an overarching vantage—both big-picture in its scope and long-term in its perspective. The first chapter provides a brief more conceptual overview. It addresses how we might best make sense of current circumstances and introduces how I think about the neces-

---

[5]   Shortly after I wrote this piece, the councilwoman I was referring to led an effort to cut the salary of the city's police chief, a black woman, by 40 percent. The chief—one of the best in the country—resigned. The councilwoman offered no apology.

sary task going forward. I will attempt to make clear that the problem is not with particular positions, but with division itself.

The eight chapters that follow address specific topics where extreme polarization is common. I chose the issues that I have because each has something particular to teach us about what the future is requiring of us. The topics: the kind of us-versus-them thinking that has historically led to war, climate change, health care reform, abortion, immigration, bigotry (in particular, sexism and racism), the disparate views of science and religion, and conflicting ways of thinking about progress. I will use these topics both to bring focus to what we find today and to provide practice in applying needed more mature approaches to decision-making.

Chapter Ten provides more in-depth conceptual perspective. It examines why we think in the language of polarity in the first place, explores in greater depth why we may be seeing the extreme polarization we witness today, and looks more closely at just how the kind of thinking needed going forward is different from what we have known in times past.

Readers could find aspects of this book's inquiry disturbing and even dispiriting. I will often bring attention to how we live in particularly dangerous times, ones in which at present we are rarely demonstrating basic sanity, much less the needed new maturity. But ultimately these reflections will be not just informative, but also hopeful. At the least, they suggest that there are ways forward—indeed, ways that in potential could be deeply rewarding.

CHAPTER ONE

Big-Picture Perspective and the Essential Task Before Us

This chapter will be a bit more conceptual than the more topic-specific chapters that follow. I ask readers who may shy away from theory to bear with me. What the book proposes is ultimately straightforward. But to get at this simplicity, we need some of the background this chapter provides. Here I will include just enough theory so that how I address particular issues in chapters ahead will make basic sense. In Chapter Ten, I will expand on these observations for those who would like more conceptual detail. For now, if the more abstract is not your cup of tea, you can skim this chapter's observations and come back to them for a closer look after you have made it a bit further into the book.

I laid the groundwork for the overarching perspective the book draws on very early in my thinking. In my 1984 book, *The Creative Imperative: Human Growth and Planetary Evolution*,[1] I described how we can think of the challenges that most define our times developmentally—in terms of a necessary "growing up" in how we think and act. My second book, *Necessary Wisdom: Meeting the Challenge of a New Cultural Maturity*

---

[1]   Charles M. Johnston, MD, *The Creative Imperative: Human Growth and Planetary Evolution,* Celestial Arts, 1984.

(1991)[2] more directly addressed the more nuanced and encompassing kind of understanding that essential questions of all sorts are requiring of us.

Of particular pertinence for this book's reflections, I structured *Necessary Wisdom* around the importance of more fully getting our minds around realities that we have always before thought of in either/or terms. I also documented how, over the course of the last century, we have witnessed initial successes with doing so. For example, we saw ecological thought beginning to heal the historical split between humankind and nature, psychology and psychiatry inviting a new appreciation of ways that conscious and unconscious might relate, and modern physics stepping beyond the once clear separation between matter and energy.

With my later, more lengthy book, *Cultural Maturity: A Guidebook for the Future*, I observed progress that we have made since with other polarities that I had noted. For example, I described how the ending of the Cold War reflected success in getting beyond the polar antagonisms that have traditionally led to war. The fact that we have not seen major conflagrations between superpowers since that time adds to the possibility that this achievement reflected real progress. I also examined the way many of the most important advances of recent decades have involved challenges to traditional leader/follower relationships. There is how, for example, in my own field of medicine, the traditional image of doctor as omniscient father figure has given way to a more humble role for the physician and a more empowered role for the patient. We have also seen limited continuing progress with some social concerns, in particular gay rights and with beginning to think more complexly about gender.

---

[2]   Charles M. Johnton, MD, *Necessary Wisdom: Meeting the Challenge of a New Cultural Maturity*, Celestial Arts, 1991.

But in both of these books I predicted that we would witness something that we have not seen—a growing ability to think more systemically about social/political issues of all sorts. In fact, over recent decades, we have often seen the opposite. In the political sphere, we have witnessed increasing polarization to the point that simple congeniality across the political aisles has largely ceased to exist. And gradually over the same time, it has become impossible around many social issues to have any kind of meaningful discussion without being ambushed by ideology. Not only have we failed to make further progress, we have witnessed significant regression. This book attempts to bring big-picture perspective to understanding what we see and the challenges ahead.

The Short Version

I've discovered in writing that it often works best, rather than waiting to put a book's conclusions at the end, to start with them—even if they won't initially make full sense. As a preview of coming attractions, here are the book's main points:

1: In recent decades we've found it increasingly difficult to get beyond assumptions that are polarized and polarizing. Indeed, we've often regressed significantly in this regard. This fact not only puts people at odds, it gets in the way of addressing the questions on which our future most depends.

2: The fact that we tend to think in the language of polarity in itself is not a problem. Doing so follows from how human understanding works, or at least how it has worked in times past.[3] And momentary periods of fairly extreme polarization have al-

---

3   We will examine Creative Systems Theory's explanation more specifically in Chapter Ten.

ways been with us.[4] But what we find today appears to reflect something different, and of more fundamental importance.

3: We tend to think of polarization in terms of conflict with regard to specific issues. But in fact it is less that issues today are creating polarization than that polarization is creating the issues—at least how we experience them. The culprit isn't even shortcomings in the more general beliefs of the Right or the Left, though there is that. Rather, it is division itself.

4: Addressing current antagonisms requires more than just meeting others halfway or even efforts at mutual understanding. Conflicting viewpoints are products of opposed ideological beliefs. More fundamentally, they are products of contrasting patterns of thought—patterns of psychological/cognitive organization. If we wish to get beyond current polarized and polarizing assumptions, we have to expand how we think and act. That means bringing more encompassing and developmentally mature—more "grown-up"—perspective to how we understand.

5: The needed greater maturity starts with the recognition that our times present new questions, many of which before now would have been too much for us to tolerate. It then quickly confronts us with how addressing those questions requires new abilities—new, more mature skills and capacities. Ultimately we face the need to draw on new, more post-ideological and em-

---

[4]   And often they have been of particular concern. For example, polarization at the time of the Civil War was more immediately consequential than what we see today, and that of the McCarthy era or that of Vietnam War times was similarly troubling.

bracing—we could say simply more "systemic"[5]—ways of making sense of our worlds.

6: Bringing larger perspective to essential questions has the potential to benefit us powerfully. Beyond helping us avoid calamity and inviting more nuanced and effective ways of thinking, it helps us leave behind distractions that today get in the way of effectively moving forward—including polarized responses. It also makes possible more complete ways of relating both to ourselves and to others (to use the language of Creative Systems Theory, more Whole-Person/Whole-System ways of understanding identity and relationship). We become able to more fully understand ourselves. We also become capable of engaging interpersonal connections of all kinds, from the most private to the most global, with a depth that has not before been an option.

7: These changes will be essential to any kind of future we would wish to be a part of. But success is in no way guaranteed. The challenges our times present may well be too much for us. The important recognition is that a way forward exists that is worthy of our courage and commitment.

I will come back to a further key observation shortly that will have a central place throughout these reflections. What getting beyond polarized thinking asks of us is neither mysterious nor ultimately complicated. There are ways in which the picture that results is not just more straightforward than what it replaces, it is ultimately simpler. In the end, the needed new picture is only about leaving behind protective

---

[5]   Creative Systems Theory uses the word "systemic" in a specific sense, to refer not to the kind of systemic thinking used by a good engineer to understand the workings of machines, but rather to thinking that draws on the whole of ourselves as systems.

simplifications and seeing more clearly what is in fact the case. We will also come back to a further recognition, one that supports the possibility that we might succeed at what is being asked. If Creative Systems Theory's developmental picture is correct, at least as potential the needed more "grown-up" ways of understanding and acting are built into who we are.

Why We See What We Do

I've observed that we have regressed with regard to many social/political concerns of late and tied the fact of increased polarization to this backsliding. In writing a book such as this, it would be ideal if I could clearly delineate the causes for such regression. At this point, the best I can do is outline some of the most likely factors. In Chapter Ten, I will go into greater detail, particularly with regard to the factors that are most directly pertinent to this book's broader contribution. The years ahead should make things more clear.

But the question of why we see what we do is definitely important. The consequences could be very different depending on the answer. And depending on our answer, what is being asked of us could also be very different. With several explanations, major changes—at least in the short term—may not be needed. But there are also reasons to think we may be dealing with dynamics of a more fundamental sort.

It is possible that the extreme polarization we witness today is a product simply of how change in social systems has always worked. Polarization does not at all require disagreement. I've hinted at how thinking in polar terms follows from how human intelligence works. There is also the two-steps-forward-one-step-back nature of change. But the degree of backsliding we witness would suggest that more than just this is at work.

It is also possible that what we witness could follow from dynamics more particular to our time but which still have familiar antidotes. Today's extreme views might reflect momentary regression in the face of today's many highly demanding challenges. It is in the nature of human systems that they will often regress when confronted with demands that threaten to overwhelm them.[6] If the challenges are temporary and the overwhelm is not that great, patience and perspective—at least if we can avoid making destructive choices in response to being over-whelmed—should be all that is needed to take care of things.

Of greater concern, what we see could also be a consequence of more ultimately overwhelming challenges and, with them, regression of a more pronounced—and less easily addressed—sort. Many of today's critical concerns—for example, globalization, climate change, job loss through automation, the dramatic changes of the information revolution, the growing gap between the world's haves and have-nots, and the loss of familiar cultural guideposts in so many areas of our lives (from generally agreed-upon moral codes to clearly defined national and religious allegiances)—are more specifically new and could result in overwhelm of a particularly severe sort. It is important to recognize that regressive dynamics over recent decades have spanned the globe. We see them in the growing prevalence of authoritarian rule in fledg-ling democracies. We also find them with the rising tide of fundamen-talism in the Islamic East. If what we witness is primarily a product of such more deeply challenging and often global dynamics, successfully moving forward could be considerably more difficult. Indeed, what effectively moving forward asks may be more than we are capable of.

Importantly, there is an observation with particular pertinence to this book's inquiry hidden in these descriptions. If it is accurate, while it doesn't make things easier, it does alter the possible implications. As-pects of this easily overwhelming picture—for example, the loss of fa-

---

6   Put in Creative Systems Theory terms, polarization is a common protec-tive mechanism when the demands made by the challenges a system con-fronts exceed its Capacitance (the amount of reality it can comfortably take in and handle). Black-and-white thinking dramatically reduces uncer-tainty and a challenge's felt complexity.

miliar guideposts in many areas of our lives—may be products of Cultural Maturity–related changes. With the topic-specific chapters ahead, we will examine how the demands that come with Cultural Maturity's "growing up" require that we face realities that before now we could not have tolerated.

If such demands are playing a major role in what we see, this would further increase what our times require of us—considerably. But it would also increase the likelihood that we can get through these difficult times. It would mean that what we are feeling overwhelmed by may be at least in part what in the end will be required to save us. Later we will examine how this possibility also suggests that we may well get through these difficult times more quickly than we might imagine. We might best think of today's backsliding as part of an awkward in-between time in a predicted developmental process.

Whether Cultural Maturity's changes contribute significantly to what we see today is impossible to know from where we sit. The concept itself can be debated. And because it is a big-picture concept, most obviously pertinent to thinking of changes over the long term, effects with regard to any particular time can really only be analyzed by looking back. But if Cultural Maturity's demands do play a significant role, that makes what we see today more understandable and also supports that hope may be warranted.

Later we will look at kinds of evidence beyond just the nature of the challenges we face that support the idea that Cultural Maturity's changes may play a role in what we see. Making full sense of them will require Chapter Ten's more detailed theoretical reflections, but they will provide important additional insight. We will examine, for example, how the degree of absurdity that we often find today can be thought of as evidence. I will also describe how the fact that today we find polarization not just between historically common competing forces such as management and labor, but between alternative extreme populist ideologies, is consistent with what the concept of Cultural Maturity would predict.

But we are getting ahead of ourselves. The important recognition in getting started is that, whatever their origins, today's extreme social and political divisions directly put us at risk. In chapters ahead we will see how the critical nature of so many of the challenges that we now confront means that such deep differences present real dangers. We will also see that, whatever the cause, what is being called for is ultimately the same—the ability to understand our worlds in more mature and encompassing ways. This is the case even if the challenge is only to weather the effects of more particular stressors. But it is certainly true if Cultural Maturity's demands are playing a significant role in what we see. More specific policy approaches could have an impact. For example, anything that begins to address today's growing economic disparities could lessen populist tensions. And, in the short term, we may get away with simply finding ways to better get along. But I will argue that with time, the need for the kind of more integrative change that comes with Cultural Maturity's "growing up" should become inescapable.

Absurdities All the Way Around

A couple of recognitions have particular importance as we dive in. I highlighted the first in the Preface, how most everyone today is playing a part in today's untenable circumstances. In recent decades, social/political polarization has become an increasingly intractable part of the social fabric on both the Right and the Left. And the situation today is becoming only more extreme.

We saw such ideological absolutism first becoming clearly entrenched on the political right in the United States in the last decade of the twentieth century with Newt Gingrich's "Contract with America," and early in this century with the Tea Party movement. We witnessed previous intimations with the candidacy of Barry Goldwater in the 80s and his assertion that "extremism in defense of liberty is no vice," and later, off and on, with the presidency of Ronald Reagan. But really extreme views were then not widely held. With the Right, today, we find the bizarre situation of having people in major positions of power in government being essentially anti-government. At the extreme, we find conspiracy-theory thinking that but a few years back could be found only in the most fringe of tabloid publications and in the darkest recesses of the Internet becoming at least entertained by mainstream figures.

These extreme views legitimately concern us. At the least, government will become only more nonfunctional if extreme anti-government sentiments from the Right continue to grow in influence. Republicans in the U.S. have made government a zero sum game in which winning at all costs is what it is all about. They have forgotten that there is a higher good—the well-being of democratic institutions. And extreme nationalistic tendencies that can accompany such absolutism do direct harm to the kind of collaboration needed for addressing issues on the world stage and in potential inflame global animosities. There is also how the growing barrage of disinformation that can come from such thinking undermines people's confidence that truths of any sort can be trusted.

We tend to think of extreme populism on the Left as more recent. Actually, the Left in the U.S. has had plenty of fringe populist movements in times well past (witness the Wobblies). But more recently, if we turn not to politics, but to academia, we find the swing to a populist extreme starting about the same time. The influence of the postmodern thread in academic thought has made anything but the most liberal of beliefs taboo in the academic world. Today, you can count the number of admitted conservatives on many university campuses on one hand.[7]

---

[7]   In a July 2020 article in the *New York Times*, columnist David Brooks chastises Harvard for the fact that only 1.5% of its faculty are conserva-

It would be easy to assume that extremism on the Left is of less concern than that of the Right. But the dangers ultimately may be just as significant. At the least, extremism on the Left undermines honest engagement and the possibility of any depth and complexity of conversation. In academia, codes of political correctness have become so entrenched that ideological trip wires await for the most minor of transgressions—ones that can end people's careers if they do not have tenure, and certainly risk their reputations even if their job is secure. Increasingly we find thinking that is embarrassingly simplistic, such as historical interpretations that make the whole of the American project—and ultimately the whole of culture's Modern Age—little more than an exercise in hypocrisy and oppression.

Today more broadly we also encounter policies advocated by the extreme Left that fail the test of basic reason—such as assertions in the immigration debate that come close to suggesting that borders themselves are a problem,[8] or current proposals with regard to policing that in effect make police the enemy and imply that it would be best to just get rid of them.[9] I find calls by the Left to "defund the police" ideologically not that different from calls by the Right to "build that wall." Arguably, such assertions reflect fringe views, but as with fringe views on the Right, with growing frequency they are being treated as legitimate.

At the Obama Foundation's 2020 annual summit, Barack Obama challenged simplistic beliefs that we too often find with "woke" culture. "There is this sense" he said, that the way to provoke change "is to be judgmental about other people and that is enough. That is not activism. That is not bringing about change. If all you are doing is casting stones, you are probably not going to get that far." A person might reasonably assume that the use of a term like "woke" is related to the

---

tives and notes that the liberal *New Republic* has less diversity of viewpoint than the conservative *National Review*.

8   Chapter Six examines this particular ideological trap.

9   See Chapter Seven.

kind of greater awareness that I describe with the concept of Cultural Maturity. This can sometimes be the case, but the term's reference when used by the modern populist left tends to be specifically ideological. Claims of "wokeness" all too often have less to do with thinking that takes us forward than with beliefs that function primarily to produce feelings of moral superiority and a sense of tribal connectedness.

Again, I am always wary of making false equivalences. But in their more exaggerated populist forms, ideological beliefs of the Left can be as absolutist as those of the Right and in similar ways risk leading to dead-end consequences. Carried to an extreme, this is the same kind of thinking that brought us the Chinese Cultural Revolution and the worst excesses of the French revolution (including Robespierre and the guillotine).[10] I don't in any way expect to see such extremes today, but it is worth putting the absurdities of some of the assertions we can hear today from the Left in historical context.

Today we find multiple forces that amplify polarization on both the Right and the Left. I've noted the role of the news media in this regard. Too often the media today consider the soap opera that results when Right and Left clash almost the definition of news. Such drama reliably attracts ears and eyeballs, but in fact it only distracts from the questions that today desperately need our attention (and that if given needed attention, would actually be news). In Chapter Nine I will address how social media today is serving to amplify division in ways that could prove particularly problematical (and that could easily defy solutions).

Another place where we confront dangerous amplification of polarized beliefs is with how advocacy can be highjacked by extremist groups. On both the Right and the Left today we see actions in the streets that may start with legitimate goals, but which then devolve into

---

[10]   Populist views on the Right and populist views on the Left are each similarly anti-authoritarian. And each, in what might seem like a contradiction, readily translates into authoritarianism. Creative Systems Theory uses the term "cross-polar" to describe this common dynamic.

anarchy. The instigators of violence tend to be fringe elements. But currently we see little interest from either the Right or the Left in calling out actions that cross this critical line.

I will not be concerned in this book with the question of whether ideological claims on the Right or the Left are more ludicrous. At one time or another, the Right or the Left can each seem most prone to going wholly off the rails. And as I've noted, my interest is not really with polarization at all. The essential recognition is that ideological beliefs of every sort, just by the nature of the kind of thought they represent, will be obstacles to what is ultimately needed going forward.

I can't be sure about whether Cultural Maturity's considerable demands play a major role in creating the craziness that we can see today with extreme views any more than I can about their role with polarization more generally. But in Chapter Ten, I will examine how the fact that views on each side today are so often not just antagonistic, but simply ludicrous, is consistent with this explanation. It turns out that at a predictable point in developmental processes of all sorts—a point that we can think of as analogous to today's time in culture—we find behaviors that are hard to think of as in any way sane. We will see how the Creative Systems Theory concept of Transitional Absurdity suggests that encountering such craziness today might be expected—indeed, that we might expect to find absurdities of a specifically populist sort as we do today.

Not Just Thinking New Things, But Thinking in New Ways

The second important recognition in getting started can be a stretch for many people, but some basic understanding is important if the observations in chapters ahead are to make full sense. In the end, ideology has less to do with what we think than how we think. Ultimately it is about something more basic even than collections of beliefs and values, what people refer to with a term like "worldview"—though that gets us a bit closer. At its most fundamental, ideology is about psychological patterns, or more precisely, patterns of cognitive organization. It is not so much that belief creates polarization, but rather that polarity's role in how we think creates polarized belief.

As a psychiatrist, in working with individuals, I am used to listening less to a person's specific words than to the underlying psychological implications. I listen to "where the person is coming from." Ultimately I'm interested in the patterns of psychological/cognitive organization that generate a person's beliefs. In my role as cultural psychiatrist, it comes naturally to listen in a similar way.

The notion that social/political polarization has more to do with our cognitive mechanisms than the real complexities of policy can easily come as a surprise. We tend to think of our opinions in terms of rationally arrived-at conclusions. And the media tends to take at face value that what a person says is generally what he or she means, or at the least that the words adequately reflect what drives the person's concerns. But the recognition that we are dealing with underlying cognitive patterns is key. It is pivotal to making sense of why getting beyond polarization can be so difficult and why efforts at civil discourse so often fail. And if the concept of Cultural Maturity is accurate, it is essential to understanding what is needed going forward.

Cognitive dynamics are not all that beliefs are about. The particulars of belief can be products of reasoned consideration. And beliefs can be influenced by numerous external factors—where we live (for example, urban versus rural), the family we grow up in, or the unique challenges our particular life may present. But belief quickly translates into psychological pattern. We can think of these patterns like "ecological niches" in the makeup of our psyches. Different kinds of social narratives fit most comfortably into particular cognitive niches.

Some of the best evidence for the conclusion that ideology has less to do with what we think than how we think can be found in the common intractableness of people's opinions. We tend to assume when people have views different from our own that the appropriate response is to engage in reasoned discussion and debate. In fact, debate rarely changes anyone's mind. As often the result is positions becoming even more entrenched.

We also find evidence in how issues that eventually become highly polarized are often not thought of in partisan terms when they first come to the public's attention. This was the case, for example, with both climate change and health care reform. There were no obvious sides to the climate change debate when the evidence first came to light. And the approach on which Obamacare was initially modeled was Republican Mitt Romney's plan in Massachusetts. We often encounter related surprises with us-versus-them antagonisms on the world stage. It turns out that wars are less often the result of major differences than we tend to assume. Think of how World War I began with the assassination of Austro-Hungarian heir Archduke Franz Ferdinand. While it was a significant event, few people had any idea it could have such world-altering consequences.

We find an important further kind of evidence in the common closeness of elections. If voting were based on the perceived intelligence of a candidate's ideas, much more often than we do, we would see general agreement as to which candidate is the most qualified. Instead, elections are most often won by a few percentage points, or less. This is what we would predict if we are dealing not just with differences of opinion, but opposite polarized cognitive patterns. Pushed to extremes, polarities split fifty-fifty, like two sides of a coin. One of the best ways to win an election if you are not really qualified is to create controversy and polarization. Because polar opposites tend to split about evenly, you should then be able to get something close to 50 percent of the vote.[11]

---

[11] Unless polarization is at work, we would expect to find whatever split matches the number of people that reach each kind of conclusion.

We also find evidence in the almost inverse relationship that exists between how informed a person is and the likelihood that the person will have strong views. If surety was a product of how thoroughly topics had been examined, we would expect the opposite. But in truth we commonly find the most adamant and shrill opinions and the most lengthy pronouncements coming from people who in fact know the least and have least to offer to a real conversation. Less information more quickly aligns with cognitive patterns. More information risks creating internal dissonance.

It turns out that if we have sufficiently nuanced conceptual tools available to us, we can make pretty accurate predictions about the ideological beliefs that we will encounter by teasing apart psychological structures and patterns.[12] What we can then predict is underlying values and narratives not particulars when it comes to specific issues, but this kind of observation can prove immensely useful. At the least, it helps make sense of otherwise confusing results—such as how people can have views that would seem not at all to be in their best interest or how often we find strange-bedfellow alliances. It also helps us appreciate what the more encompassing kind of understanding that comes with culturally mature systemic perspective involves and just what it requires of us.

---

[12] Creative Systems Theory's framework provides perspective for making such discernments. It delineates how the available psychological "niches" change as a product of time in culture. The theory also includes a detailed framework for understanding temperament differences, the Creative Systems Personality Typology. The typology describes how we can understand much of what we find at specific points in time in terms of the particular ways in which various personality styles organize experience. Combine temperament as described by the framework with a person's Capacitance and we get a pretty good predictor of social/political inclinations. In *Creative Systems Theory*, I go into detail about how such patterning dynamics interplay.

Culturally Mature Understanding

Each of the book's topic-specific chapters will provide more specific illustration of how the challenge going forward has less to do with what we think than how we think. And each will more concretely demonstrate how neither Right, Left, nor somewhere in between are the only options—and can't be if we are to make today's needed more mature kinds of discernments. Each chapter's explorations will also help clarify how more is possible. My hope is that by engaging this wide array of issues, the book's inquiry will help readers build the cognitive muscles needed to address the demanding and complex concerns before us.

For the task of getting beyond current political animosities, the simple recognition that we find important contributions and also significant blindnesses on both the Right and the Left can provide a start. At least this works if the accurate diagnosis with current absurdities is that we have momentarily regressed—if what is needed is simply to get back on track. But it can provide a place to begin even if the task is of the more fundamental sort described by the concept of Cultural Maturity.

Each polar vantage advocates for values and conclusions that can contribute going forward and also beliefs that have the potential to do significant harm when applied in shortsighted ways. For example, on the Right we find a deep valuing of family, community, and country; an emphasis on personal responsibility; and particular attention given to the moral dimension. But we also find tendencies toward an overly protective and easily reactive nationalism that could be our undoing, and often a narrowness of belief that can translate into intolerance and bigotry. On the Left we find greater openness to new options and also a commitment to supporting the less advantaged. But we also find a lack of appreciation for tradition. And we find difficulty recognizing when either boundaries or leadership of a more hierarchical sort have important roles in needed solutions.

But each topic-specific chapter will also make clear that more than just this is required. Combining the best from the Right and from the Left and throwing out what fails to serve us by itself still leaves us short of what is needed. Real progress eventually hinges on appreciating the larger questions that before now would have overwhelmed us. And it requires thinking in more complete ways, engaging that needed new developmental step in how we hold experience and make sense of our worlds.

It helps to think of the changes that produce culturally mature understanding in two steps (though each, in fact, is an aspect of the same mechanism). First, Cultural Maturity involves a new, more mature kind of relationship between culture and the individual. In times past, societal beliefs and structures, by providing clear rules to live by and mythologized images of collective identity, have served like parents to the lives of individuals. With Cultural Maturity's changes, we take a more final kind of responsibility for our personal and collective actions. We also assume a fullness of authority in our lives that has not before been needed or possible.

Cultural Maturity is also a product of developmentally predicted cognitive changes. The term that Creative Systems Theory uses to describe the result of these changes—Integrative Meta-perspective—is a bit of a mouthful. But it quite precisely captures what is being asked. For this book's purpose, we can put what these cognitive changes involve simply. They challenge us to at once more fully step back from, and more deeply engage, all of who we are. More specifically, they challenge us to at once step back from and more deeply engage the whole of cognition's complexity, all the various aspects of how we understand.

One consequence of these changes has special importance for this book's reflections. We begin to leave behind our historical tendency to identify with particular parts of our internal complexity, the dynamic that before has produced ideological thinking. In the process, we also begin to get beyond the complementary need to project parts of that complexity that we may find less than pleasant onto others—the dynamic that underlies polar animosities. With Integrative Meta-perspective, we become capable of thinking about complexities of all sorts in ways that are more embracing, more of a whole. This includes both our own internal complexities and complexities in the world around us. In the process, we become better able to see things just as they are, without the protective distortions of times past.

With Chapter Ten, we will look more closely at the cognitive reordering that underlies Cultural Maturity's changes, but the general kind of change we find with Cultural Maturity is not wholly foreign to us. We witness something similar with the mature stages in individual psychological development. It is what makes it possible in our later years to be not just intelligent, but wise—at least if we successfully take on the pertinent developmental tasks. The essential difference with Cultural Maturity is that here the new step in our cognitive development is happening in our relationship not just to our experience as individuals, but in relationship to our experience as cultural beings.

To avoid confusion, it is important to distinguish what we find with Cultural Maturity from a couple of more familiar kinds of change processes. Some changes that people today might promote are best thought of as extensions of Modern Age accomplishments. For example, we can understand much in current gender- and race-related advocacy in this way. The most obvious part of the objective in each case—the achievement of equal rights and equal opportunity—while essential, reflects a further manifestation of the kind of advancement that centuries back gave us the Bill of Rights. I will argue in Chapter Seven that the kind of progress needed to effectively get beyond current bigotries also requires further steps that become possible only with Cultural Maturity's changes. I will also highlight an important reason for making this distinction. If we stop with the first kind of change, we may get greater equality, but at the same time, we are likely ultimately to see an exacerbation of conflict.

We also need to distinguish what our times require from changes that come with thinking of a more postmodern sort. I've noted how postmodern thought has had an important role in academia in recent decades. It gets us part of the way. Like the concept of Cultural Maturity, it highlights the fact that historically reliable truths no longer serve us as they have in times past. But postmodern thought, with its different-strokes-for-different-folks conclusions, gives us little of substance to replace what it insightfully takes away. It thus too easily leaves us wandering aimlessly—at a time when what people most hunger for is a sense of direction they can trust. In contrast, Cultural Maturity's cognitive reordering provides a new guiding story and new capacities needed to make our way.[13]

Images and Metaphors

Over the years, I've drawn on a variety of images and metaphors to help communicate what Integrative Meta-perspective involves and just where it takes us. Each of the main ones I've drawn on has its particular strengths and weaknesses. As several of them will prove of particular value in the chapters ahead, I will take time here for some brief descriptions. Note that when it comes to culturally mature understanding, we should expect the task of communication to be a challenge. It is not really possible to make sense of changes of a developmental sort unless a person has already made a solid start with such changes. Think of how hard it is for a child to appreciate the reality of an adolescent even if told about it in detail.[14]

---

[13] *Creative Systems Theory* fills out these distinctions and also addresses how the result with Cultural Maturity's changes is different from multiple other more common ways of thinking about the future.

[14] In fact, it is not just that we are dealing with a developmental process that produces this difficulty. Creative Systems Theory describes how the more

In *Necessary Wisdom*, I spoke in terms of "bridging" polarities. Framing Cultural Maturity's task in this way provides a simple approach. While the term "bridging" can be misinterpreted—a person could imagine that the word suggests only finding agreement or compromise[15]—when sufficiently filled out, it helps us grasp some essential understandings that are hard to get at in other ways.

A characteristic of how polar opposites in human systems relate—the fact that they reflect a predictable kind of symmetry—is key to making sense of the role of polarity in how we think. Polarities tend to juxtapose some harder, more "right-hand" quality that is concerned most with difference with some softer, more "left-hand" quality that is more concerned with connectedness—such as with war versus peace, objective versus subjective, or prose versus poetry.[16] Psychology uses language drawn from the study of myth to describe these contrasting qualities. It speaks of some qualities as being more "archetypally masculine" and others as more "archetypally feminine." Some people may find the gender-linked language bothersome as we attempt to get beyond past gender stereotypes, but it proves very helpful for making sense of polarity in human systems. Of particular importance, it points toward the dynamic way that polarities relate, how they work together in ways that are ultimately "procreative."

---

complete kind of understanding that comes with the mature stages of any development process, just by the apples-and-oranges nature of the complexity it reflects, defies conventional depiction. The theory calls this the Dilemma of Representation.

15   I will always put the word "bridging" in quotes to emphasize the difference between what the term refers to and these very different consequences.

16   With certain juxtapositions that we might think of as polarities, this is not the case. Some, like success versus failure, involve opposites in which one option is explicitly preferable. Other polarities simply reflect competing priorities that need to be balanced—as with contrasting ways we might choose to use our time. But more often, particularly when we are dealing

Over the course of the book, I will draw on several major implications of this way of thinking. One is central to Creative Systems Theory's evolutionary view of culture. An appreciation for this generative symmetry helps us understand polarity's role in developmental processes. Over the course of history, we find polarity evolving from juxtapositions that give greatest emphasis to connectedness and the archetypally feminine (as with tribal societies), to polarities where difference and the archetypally masculine has the much greater influence (as with the emphasis on materialism and competition in modern times). Creative Systems Theory describes how we find a similar kind of progression over the course of any kind of human generative process—be it a simple creative act, the course of individual human development, or how human relationships evolve.[17]

There is a way that a recognition of underlying symmetry benefits us that will prove particularly useful in chapters ahead. It helps us make sense of why social/political polarization takes the forms that it does. Commentator Chris Wallace once referred to the Democratic and Republican parties in the United States metaphorically as the "mommy party" and the "daddy party." The observation makes at least a good general shorthand for teasing apart patterns and helps us see how ideological beliefs with regard to particular issues might take the forms that they do.

This approach also provides benefit in a particularly powerful way conceptually. It helps us appreciate the workings of polarity at its most basic—what ultimately underlies division with specific issues. Creative Systems Theory makes an observation with radical implications. While we tend to think of polarity in terms of opposing positions, at its most fundamental polarity instead juxtaposes distinction and difference on one hand with connectedness and oneness on the other. Over the

---

with human systems, polarities reflect systemic aspects. It is here that the concept of "bridging" becomes pertinent.

course of the book, I will touch on multiple ways this observation is relevant to the tasks ahead.[18] And in Chapter Ten, we will examine it more conceptually. One practical implication is how it alerts us to the fact that when we confuse oneness with systemic completeness, we are quite specifically taking sides.[19]

In *Necessary Wisdom*, I used this underlying symmetry to develop a language for the various ways that understanding can stop short of the needed new sophistication. What Creative Systems Theory calls Separation Fallacies fall off of the right, more archetypally masculine side of the conceptual roadway. Unity Fallacies fall off the left, more archetypally feminine side. And with Compromise Fallacies, people walk down the middle of the road (with mediocre-middle thinking and the risk of being hit by traffic going both ways the common result).

While I've frequently found the metaphor of "bridging" useful, it is also the case that it has often proved to be less effective than I had originally hoped. People will tend to associate the image with averaging or lumping together even after I have carefully emphasized traps and fallacies. At times in using it I've simply thrown up my hands. In another way, we confront how the challenge is not just to reach new conclusions, but to think in new ways.

---

17   See *The Creative Imperative* or *Creative Systems Theory*.

18   One is how it can help us make sense of fundamental conceptual quandaries. For example, in Chapter Eight I describe how it helps us think in more encompassing ways about the relationship between science and spirituality.

19   This recognition adds a further level to the particular challenges that the tasks ahead can present for those on the political left. Because those on the Left tend to think in ways that have them identify with unity and connectedness, they can be particularly blind to their bigotries. The missing awareness is that to identify with unity is ultimately to identify with division—and, in the end, to further it. Because people on the Left rarely recognize this fact, having real conversation can be difficult. It is not possible to "agree to disagree" unless one can appreciate the fact of difference and not make difference itself an enemy.

More often today I draw on a more differentiated, but still basic image: a simple box of crayons.[20] The box represents the ability to step back and see a larger picture. The crayons represent our multihued complexity. The box-of-crayons image has a couple of particular strengths. The crayons' multiple colors remind us that with most issues there are more than just two valid "sides."[21] The image also highlights how the task has less to do with the differing viewpoints than with how we hold them. The crayons are important, but the encompassing box is what makes culturally mature understanding possible.

The box-of-crayons image provides a more visual way to depict the polar traps that I just described and helps further tie them to polarity at its most fundamental. Separation Fallacies reflect the worldviews of crayons that identify more with difference and distinction—perhaps a more conservative or more materialistic part of us. Unity Fallacies reflect the worldviews of crayons that identify with oneness or connectedness—perhaps a more liberal or more spiritual part of us. Compromise Fallacies merge opposite hued crayons, leaving us at best with a muddy brown.

I will often also draw on a third way of thinking about what is required in chapters ahead. It is less a metaphor than an approach. CST includes a number of hands-on methods that help people address issues from a more encompassing perspective. The most powerful I call simply Parts Work. In doing Parts Work, the person (or group if I am working with more than one person) envisions the various aspects of the question that concerns them like characters in a play. The person leads from his or her Whole-Person/Whole-System (culturally mature

---

[20]   I used this metaphor as the central concept in my recent book *Rethinking How We Think: Integrative Meta-Perspective and the Cultural "Growing Up" on Which Our Future Depends* (ICD Press, 2020).

[21]   Creative Systems Theory emphasizes that the fact that historically we might have thought otherwise is specifically a product of how understanding of times past has been organized in the language of polarity.

perspective) chair and engages the various parts, set in chairs around the room, in conversation about the issue at hand. If Parts Work is done well, the technique gives almost no choice but to bring the needed more mature and systemic understanding to bear.

My comprehensive work, *Creative Systems Theory,* describes the approach in depth and provides numerous examples. Here I will use Parts Work primarily as a point of reference, but even when applied in this more limited way, it adds considerably to understanding. Parts Work follows three cardinal rules. Each rule informs a particular aspect of culturally mature understanding. In chapters ahead, we will see how together they get at where Integrative Meta-perspective takes us in a way that is at once directly graspable and precise.

Rule #1—*The Whole-Person chair (or Whole-System perspective chair with larger cultural issues) provides the leadership in a culturally mature reality.* It is the Whole-Person chair that interacts with the world. And the Whole-Person chair, through interacting with each of the parts, draws on their contributions. This rule makes doing Parts Work a hands-on exercise for practicing culturally mature leadership—in oneself and in the world.

Rule #2—*Parts don't interact with the world.* A person doing Parts Work quickly recognizes that engaging the world from parts, while it is what most people do the larger portion of the time, produces limited and limiting results. People also come to recognize that ideological beliefs—whether political, religious, or those of competing belief systems within their particular professions—involve parts taking over and acting as if they have a relationship with the world.

Rule #3—*Parts don't talk to parts.* This recognition can take a bit longer to grasp, but it is ultimately just as critical. We can think of much in the internal struggles of daily life as crosstalk between competing parts. And the implications are just as significant collectively. Parts talking to parts can have us confuse moderation or compromise with culturally mature perspective. In addition, ideological beliefs of the less extreme sort often have their roots in parts talking to parts. In *Creative*

Systems Theory, I describe how we can understand the back and forth between competing worldviews over the course of history as a similar kind of conversation between systemic parts.

We can think of the result with Parts Work as a kind of "cognitive rewiring." Wires are cut between both parts and the world, and between parts. At the same time, people strengthen the wires that run between themselves and the world, and also between themselves and their diverse and variously creative and contributing parts. Key to the power of the Parts Work approach is that the person does not need to be conscious of why it is working. Get the wiring right and culturally mature perspective is an inherent result.

With this book's topic-specific chapters, I will frequently draw on Parts Work and the rewiring image in a specific way. When I do Parts Work with an individual, I have the person (sitting in the Whole-Person/Whole-System perspective leadership chair) articulate "yeses and nos" with regard to each part—state clearly where each part can be helpful and also where it is ultimately unhelpful. At some point in topic-specific chapters, after identifying the new defining question, I will take time to delineate some of the specific yeses and nos that the Whole-Person/Whole-System perspective chair must make with regard to ideological conclusions that have before divided responses with regard to that specific topic.

Parts Work highlights a recognition essential to fully grasping the point of this book. While these introductory reflections have most emphasized the dangers of extreme viewpoints, culturally mature perspective in the end challenges not just views of an extreme sort, but also the most commonplace of traditional beliefs. With regard specifically to the ideological assumptions of the Right and the Left, it confronts even those of a tempered sort. Framed in the language of Parts Work, while we have problems if an extreme part takes over, in the end, we have stopped just as short of culturally mature understanding if the most moderate and well-meaning of parts ends up running the show.

Besides applying these specific tools, with each of the book's topic-specific chapters, I will also draw on a way of thinking about Cultural Maturity's cognitive changes that can be thought of as following from any of them. I've noted how effectively engaging the important questions before us will require new kinds of skills and capacities. We will see how this is the case with each of the topics we will address. A key example is the importance of assuming a more ultimate kind of responsibility. We will look at how the tasks ahead require not just that we be more responsible for our choices, but also that we be newly responsible for the truths on which we base our choices. Other key new capacities include finding greater comfort with complexity and uncertainty, better tolerating limits, and understanding how truths of all sorts exist in a context. All these new abilities are things we can practice. But it is also the case that they follow naturally from Cultural Maturity's cognitive reordering. We do not need to create them from whole cloth.[22]

As some of these ways of thinking about Cultural Maturity's changes might seem a bit abstract, I will offer one more metaphor that in a simple way brings us back more specifically to Right versus Left antagonisms and helps fill out what is needed. We can think of worldviews of the more liberal sort as like the gas pedal on a car; views of a more conservative sort like the brake. As we conventionally think about polarity, we end up with an ultimately silly question: Which is more important? Obviously each has a purpose and serves us when the time is right. But there are also further ingredients necessary to driving effectively. There is the steering wheel. There is also the importance of learning to drive skillfully and wisely. And certainly we need to be able to discern the right direction to go. In these pages, I will give attention to the fact of polarization and how the sensibilities that most ally with each pole—as with the gas pedal and the brake—have their times and

---

22   I organized two of my books, *Cultural Maturity: A Guidebook for the Future* and *Hope and the Future: Confronting Today's Crisis of Purpose* around these

places. But I will be most concerned with these further ingredients. They are what moving forward collectively in the most safe and wise manner—including using the gas and brake as needed—will ultimately require of us.

A Needed New Common Sense

With each of the issues that topic-specific chapters ahead take on, we will encounter what at first might seem a paradox. I pointed toward it earlier and promised to return for a closer look. While Cultural Maturity's changes require that we think in ways that are more complex and nuanced than the more ideological worldviews of times past, at the same time they produce understanding that is in important ways more ordinary than what we have known—indeed, simpler. This result follows naturally from where Cultural Maturity's changes take us.

The complexity side of things will most stand out with how each topic calls into question familiar ideological beliefs. I will give greatest attention in this regard to the ideological beliefs of the political right and the political left, and in particular to their more extreme forms. It is simply true that today it is rare for people not to identify ultimately with the conclusions of the Right or the Left. But I will also make reference to truths of a more ideological sort that may have their origins in religion, philosophy, science, or the technological. Most readers should not find this a concern with ideological beliefs that they disagree with (though I will often propose that the problem with the offending belief is likely different than one assumes). But just as fundamentally, required steps will challenge assumptions that may be some of the reader's most cherished. There will be no escape from this fate.

The simplicity side of things may not be so obvious, but there are reasons why it too might be expected. For example, while today we tend to assume that it is differences that most define us—and too often

---

needed new skills and capacities.

differences of an absolute polar sort—in my experience, when it comes to the things that people most care about, we have much more in common than not. Get a dozen people in a room and talk about values and what to them most ultimately matters, and we find answers that are surprisingly similar. It is reasonable to think that if we can bring a more encompassing and complete kind of perspective to our understanding, we will find something that reflects a less dramatic, more ordinary-feeling kind of reality.

I've made reference to the simplicity side of things more conceptually in claiming that while culturally mature perspective demands a lot of us—indeed, more than we've before been capable of—in the end, it is only about better seeing what is in fact the case. Appreciating this result requires that we perceive with a completeness that before now would have been too much to handle. But in the end, culturally mature understanding is only about seeing what is right before us more accurately.

We can also appreciate this simpler, less dramatic result by contrasting it with other interpretations of what may lie ahead. I sometimes joke, only partly tongue-in-cheek, that "normal" has become the new radical. I don't have any problem with radical positions, even of the most extreme sort. Historically, radical positions have opened our eyes to social factors we may have ignored and served to expand the conversation in essential ways.[23] But the concept of Cultural Maturity directly parts ways with current radical claims when they advocate for extreme truths that call on us to fight to the death for their realization. Most obviously such claims then fail us because they set us against one

---

[23] As far as the radical viewpoints that will here most often provide contrast, current more conservative extremist views in the U.S. have alerted us to the depth of alienation and discontent that today resides in major parts of America. The extremes of liberal populism have similarly brought new attention to racial injustice and social inequities.

another and often put us at risk. But I will argue, too, that they fail us because they aren't sufficiently radical.

I've noted how populist views are often put forward today as if they are "big ideas." Rarely in fact do they offer anything that is really new. And inevitably they miss where the truly big—and essential—questions in fact lie. In the chapters ahead, we will see how we have no choice but to begin to engage a more authentic kind of radical task, one that makes today's more reactive kinds of radicalism at best trivial, at worst diversions from what is ultimately being asked of us. If Right and Left are each failing to ask the important questions, then finding truth in extreme versions of one or the other only takes our attention away from the real—truly radical—task at hand.

Bringing culturally mature perspective to today's important questions might still seem like an impossibly complex endeavor, and in the sense that it challenges us to think in new ways, certainly it asks a lot. But each more topic-specific chapter will in a different way argue for the conclusion that culturally mature understanding is really rather common sense, just a more fully grown-up kind of common sense than we are used to. And we can get to the same conclusion without any knowledge of issues. If one thinks about it, the fact that today we've come to regard Right and Left as not just different, but opposite and mutually exclusive, is rather nonsensical. Wouldn't it be much more reasonable to assume that reality is in some way whole and that our task is to understand just how this might be so? Before now this so-phistication of common sense would have only overwhelmed and confused us. But, today, our future well-being—and perhaps our survival—depends on it.[24]

------

[24]   I've noted that the meeting of complexity and simplicity that these obser-vations point toward might at first seem a paradox. I used the phrase "at first," because in the end this result is not paradoxical, just how things work when we engage experience with the needed, more systemic per-spective. In observing that the pistons in a car's engine go up and down

The eight chapters immediately ahead will each bring attention to both the complexity and the simplicity aspects of what our times demand. With each chapter, I will also take things a bit further and expand its particular insights to address a few more encompassing concerns. I may also extend insights into the future—indeed, often well into the future. It is not important that the reader agree with these further reflections or even find them making sense. If nothing else, they will help illustrate how addressing issues systemically can result in new recognitions and unexpected possibilities. In each case, these will be ideas that would not occur to a person whose thinking was limited to polarized and polarizing assumptions.

The Next Ten to Twenty Years

What should we expect in the years immediately ahead? In the U.S., at least in the short term, it is quite possible that we will witness a diminishing of the craziness from both sides. We now have leadership of a more down-to-earth and generally sane sort. We could well see a certain "righting of the ship." And a great deal could be accomplished in the U.S. just through reinstating many of the forward-thinking policies that were eliminated by the outgoing administration.

There is a good reason to be happy with such a "good enough" result even if it often remains short of what a more culturally mature kind of advocacy might propose. A second kind of scenario is just as possible—a further amplification of extreme ideological tendencies from both the Right and Left. The outcome could be even more widespread social discord. And we could see effective governance becoming essentially impossible. While my best guess is that we will at least start with a

---

while the car goes forward, this could seem a paradox if one had not before encountered an engine. In a related way, once we at all deeply engage Cultural Maturity's changes, we see that there is no contradiction in the fact that in better holding understanding's complexity we encounter an ultimately simpler world. One recognition follows directly from the other.

period of greater sanity, if how I think about current underlying change processes is accurate, it is very likely that eventually we will witness further exacerbation of discord in some form. I've emphasized that the forces driving polarization are affecting everyone on the planet. If we don't handle such conflict wisely, the results could be badly destabilizing.

But there is also the possibility that we might see changes that are more directly pertinent to observations in this book. We could use the challenges we face—and with them the underlying sensibilities that today so easily come into conflict—to help us learn to lead and think in more systemic, more "grown-up," ways. This result is not wholly incompatible with either of the other scenarios I have described. A period of righting the ship could give us just enough of a pause that we could prepare ourselves for the more challenging tasks ahead and have time to better grasp just what is being asked. And a period of increasing disorder and discord could have the effect of alerting us to the dangers that ideological absolutisms of all sorts present and how fundamentally they leave us short of what is needed. If the concept of Cultural Maturity is correct, the further kind of change it describes must define our task eventually—and if the decades ahead are not to be brutishly unpleasant, it must do so sooner rather than later.

It is impossible to know just what the years immediately before us will bring. And there is even less we can know for sure when it comes to centuries ahead. I can imagine our future at times being at best very rough going. I can also imagine scenarios in which culturally mature capacities play an increasingly important role. Personally, I don't see how it is possible to be legitimately hopeful about the future if they do not. I've written this book to support engaging the human challenges ahead in ways that are most consistent with this more affirming outcome.

CHAPTER TWO

War and Peace—Confronting Our Historical Need for Enemies

Not too long ago it was polar battles between "hawks" and "doves" that most clearly divided conservative and liberal thinking. Today such antagonisms are more often replaced by polarization that separates us around social issues. But depending on world circumstances, the way Right and Left can polarize with questions of war and peace could easily once again move to the fore and dominate the partisan debate.

I begin the book's more topic-specific observations with this particular polarity in part because it is here that the inability to reconcile differences could most easily lead to our demise. But I also start here because of how well the topic sets the stage for addressing the concerns of later chapters. Of particular importance, it helps us answer the important question of just how the polarized thinking of times past has served us. In addition, it further supports the conclusion that the fact of polarization has more to do with how we think than what we think. And perhaps surprisingly, it also helps us with understanding how it might be legitimate to feel hopeful as we look to the future.

To fully appreciate these various results, we need to briefly set aside conflicts between Right and Left and take some time with a more basic kind of polarity—that which creates the dynamics of war to begin with.

The beliefs that most contribute to war have less to do with partisan sensibilities than with how the world looks when culture's function is parental. Historically, we've tended to divide our world into allies and enemies—"chosen people" and "evil others." This more basic polarity gives us this chapter's essential overarching question: Is it possible to have social identity without having enemies?

It is important to appreciate that while chosen-people/evil-other thinking can have less-than-pleasant consequences, historically it has benefitted us. Most immediately, it has protected us from a major portion of life's easily overwhelming complexities and uncertainties. Us-versus-them thinking reduces a multifaceted, multihued, often contradictory world to a more manageable black and white. There is also a related, more specific result that has particular importance when it comes to the dynamics that have historically led to war. Chosen-people beliefs have provided a secure, unquestioned sense of collective identity.

But as important as understanding the benefits of seeing our world in ally-versus-enemy terms is recognizing that continuing to do so has ceased to be an option. With weapons of mass destruction more and more available not just to nations but to rogue states and terrorist groups, the possibility of catastrophic outcomes has never been higher. And the fact that addressing so many of the most critical challenges ahead for us as a species will require global cooperation—climate change, divisive economic disparities, and the risks of pandemic to name just a few—further amplifies the risks of thinking in ways that separate the world's people into opposing camps. If we are to have a world that works for anyone, it is essential that we learn to relate collectively in more mature ways.

Our historical need for us-versus-them thinking brings us back to my assertion in the previous chapter that polarized beliefs have to do not just with what we think, but how we think. There I used as evidence the example of how often wars are less the result of major differences than we might assume. Once us-versus-them dynamics are set in motion, they easily take on a life of their own. Our historical need to think in us-versus-them terms also helps us better understand the process that produces what we see. When we divide our worlds into allies and enemies, we identify with an idealized part of our whole-box-of-crayons complexity and project an unconscious negative part onto others. The absolutism we bring to how we view both our own kind and those we denigrate follows predictably from this cognitive mechanism.

Many people would argue that getting beyond chosen-people/evil-other thinking is really not possible, that we have evolved to be warlike, and that is that. Given today's realities, if this is the case we can stop our inquiry right here—we are doomed. Creative Systems Theory argues that fortunately this is not the case. It proposes that at least the potential to take needed further steps is built into what makes us human.

But before we turn to how this might be so, it is important to note that recent events support the conclusion that hope may well be warranted. At the very least we are better recognizing how us-versus-them dynamics have ceased to benefit us as they once did. When Richard Nixon was president in the U.S., he uttered these chilling words: "It may seem melodramatic to say that the United States and Russia represent Good and Evil, Light and Darkness, God and the Devil. But if we think of it that way, it helps clarify our perspective in the world struggle." When we now look back, we appropriately feel fortunate that such sentiments did not result in truly unfortunate outcomes.

It is also the case that getting beyond our past need to see the world in terms of allies and enemies is something we are beginning to see. I think immediately of the fall of the Berlin Wall. Few anticipated it, certainly not the suddenness of its collapse. And while leaders have taken credit for it, at least as I see things, political initiatives didn't in fact have that much to do with the event. The cause was at once simpler and more profound. In effect, we got bored with what the wall

represented. The absoluteness of belief and the knee-jerk polar animosities needed to support it stopped being sufficiently compelling.

More recently, while we have had ample opportunity to engage in
evil-other thinking, we have tended not to fall for the bait. The 9/11
World Trade Center attacks provided every reason to make terrorism
the new communism and in the process undermine any possibility of
effectively addressing it. Or worse, we could have made the Islamic
East the new "evil empire" and turned predicted new uncertainties into
a clash of civilizations. But while leaders have sometimes played the
demon card, to a remarkable degree average citizens have not. Most
people today see terrorism as complex and dreadful, but not a product
of people who are themselves inherently evil. Seen from a historical
vantage, this fact is striking. Seen in relation to the question of whether
we are up to what the future more broadly will require, it provides important encouragement.

I promised to return to the claim that the potential for a needed
next step in how we think about identity—and in this case in particular,
collective identity—is built into our human natures. Creative Systems
Theory proposes that the ability to get beyond thinking of identity in
chosen-people/evil-other terms follows directly from how developmental processes work. More specifically, it follows from Cultural Maturity's notion of a now possible cognitive "growing up." With
Cultural Maturity's cognitive changes, we become newly able to leave
behind projective dynamics, and with this, to engage relationships of all
sorts from a more Whole-person/Whole-System place. When we do,
we come to see our past need for chosen people and evil others as
something that may once have been developmentally important (and
whose heroic stories we can still legitimately look back on and value)
but that today, along with putting us at risk, also gets in the way of us
being fully who we are. Reflexively viewing the world in ally and enemy
terms comes to feel like a historical artifact—and a dangerous one.

This recognition provides a good segue for turning to the ideological beliefs of the political right and the political left—the kind of chosen-people/evil-other thinking that is the more specific focus with this book. In how we have allied in hawks-versus-doves warring camps in times past, we find added support for the conclusion that what we see has more to do with how we think than what is in fact the case. If we step back, we recognize that there is no absolute line dividing more aggressive and more diplomatic approaches on the world stage, only the line we make in our thinking. And the particular beliefs of the Right and the Left provide further hints as far as what moving forward necessarily involves. Neither the Right nor the Left (nor just a position somewhere in between) is capable of producing the needed Whole-Person/Whole-System perspective. The Right, certainly in its more simplistic manifestations, has a hard time getting beyond a narrow nationalism. And the Left, in too easily just siding with peace, fails to recognize what real peace requires and too readily becomes in its own way just as polemical and ideological.

I remember confronting the importance of grasping a larger picture in my twenties when opposing the Vietnam War. I recognized then that while I was very much against the war, I was not ultimately anti-war. Historically, we have been put at risk both by leaders who have been too quick to go to war and by leaders who have hesitated when strong responses were needed—as with the rise of fascism prior to the Second World War. As we look to the future, the risks associated with each kind of failing become multiplied many times over. It is clear that we live in a time in which war of any scale has simply become untenable. But it is just as clear that any kind of peace that can work going forward requires an ability and willingness to defend that peace. What culturally mature leadership provides is the ability to make the necessary, often highly nuanced and systemically complex decisions wisely.

The kind of thinking needed to effectively engage questions of war and peace requires that both the Right and the Left as we have known them surrender familiar assumptions. And at the same time, as we would predict, it also draws on the best of sensibilities from both sides. We can use the Parts Work analogy to help clarify both the limitations and the contributions. The no to the Right emphasizes that having enemies can't continue to work as a means of self-definition. The yes to the Right affirms that local identity is important and can continue to exist only with protection. The no to the Left emphasizes that focusing only on peace ignores the importance of standing for essential values and the role of boundaries in the healthy functioning of systems. The yes to the Left affirms the power of diplomacy and the importance of a more encompassing picture of identity.

The challenge of getting beyond us-versus-them thinking on the global stage also provides good illustration of the importance of how Cultural Maturity's changes make possible essential new skills and capacities. Each of those I've noted—a willingness to take on a more ultimate kind of responsibility, greater comfort with complexity and uncertainty, the ability to better tolerate limits, and the understanding that truths of all sorts exist in a context—is pertinent.

I've described how Cultural Maturity's cognitive changes make us responsible at a whole new level for the truths we draw on both personally and collectively. We see the importance of this ultimate kind of responsibility with questions of war and peace in how Integrative Meta-perspective challenges us to leave behind our past need to find identity in mythologized, parental notions of culture. The truths we draw on to define ourselves and others become ours to determine in a fundamentally new sense.

I've also observed how a primary function of chosen-people/evil-other beliefs has been to protect us from complexity and uncertainty. Integrative Meta-perspective, by helping us more fully step back from and also more deeply engage our internal cognitive complexities, helps us better tolerate—indeed, find fascination and purpose in—a world that is similarly complex and where what we can know for sure is often much less than we might prefer.

The importance of better tolerating limits manifests in multiple ways that provide insight for understanding limits more generally. The old Modern Age story was heroic. Heroic narratives proclaim that the task when we encounter limits is to break through them. Culturally mature perspective alerts us to the fact that some limits are inviolable and makes clear that when we ignore this fact we pay a high price. While the importance of acknowledging real limits will come most obviously to the fore with topics we will address in future chapters such as climate change and the need to confront economic limits with health care, it plays just as fundamental a role with questions of war and peace.

Of most obvious importance, we confront limits to the ability of past beliefs to support identity, both limits to the ability of chosen-people associations to affirm the specialness—indeed, sacredness—of who we are and limits to the ability of evil-other associations to assure us about who we are not. Better tolerating the fact of real limits also has direct pertinence to the recognition that traps on the Right and on the Left each put us at risk. The Modern Age story is not just heroic; it is at once heroic and romantic. Heroic and romantic narratives (we could say more right-hand and more left-hand narratives) each deny limits, but in opposite ways. While heroic narratives actively challenge limits, romantic narratives magically dissolve them, whether through a kiss, or as with war and peace, through an idealized identification with equanimity and connectedness. With Modern Age belief we proclaim ours to be "a time without limits." Integrative Meta-perspective takes us beyond limits-denying stories of both the heroic and romantic sorts and helps us appreciate how, in real life, limits come with the territory.

The final new capacity concerns the fact that what is true often depends on when and where you look. In times past, any deep recognition of the importance of context would have similarly been more than we could handle. With Integrative Meta-perspective we see that addressing questions of context becomes essential. And the deeper connection with our own inner complexities makes it newly possible to make the needed more context-specific discernments.

An example of the importance of being attentive to context—here contextual relativity in time—concerns ways that Culturally Maturity's changes add further layers to broader cultural responsibilities. Creative Systems Theory describes how not all places on the planet reside at the same place developmentally. One consequence is that in a global world those who are furthest along necessarily become responsible for providing broader leadership. Another is that we should not expect relating in a culturally mature way to necessarily be met with a similarly mature response. Given that culturally mature leadership itself makes considerable demands, this might seem rather unfair. But in fact we know this additional kind of responsibility from other developmental processes. We don't expect adolescents to act like adults, and we realize in moments when we may catch ourselves demanding that they do that we ourselves are not acting maturely

Grasping the Larger Task

So what exactly does getting beyond an allies-versus-enemies reality look like—and feel like? This simple question could not be more important. Its answer isn't obvious from usual ways of thinking. And finding ways to answer it effectively will be increasingly essential not just if we are to avoid dangers at a global scale, but also if we are to effectively address the more immediate evil-other/chosen-people dynamics that we find between advocates for the political right and the political left.

In asking this question, I'm drawn back to an interaction from my childhood. At first the experience might seem rather minor, particularly in the context of concerns as momentous as war and peace. But for the question of how we might learn to think differently, it begins to point toward an answer.

I would often join my uncle, who lived next door, to watch football games on television, in part just to hang out with him, but also to learn more about the game. These being the days before Seattle had a team, I remember struggling to figure out who to root for, sometimes even consulting a map to figure out which city was closer to ours. I remember once asking my uncle how he decided which side to root for—and being startled by his response. He answered that he really didn't pick sides, that he really just enjoyed a good game.

I'm not sure if he would have given the same answer if there had then been a team in Seattle. And I am not at all suggesting that being dispassionate is the right way to watch a football game. What draws me back to the story is how wholly incomprehensible I then found his response. Today, I very much enjoy a good game. And I am happy to share in the camaraderie of rooting for the local team. But it is also the case that in watching a game I often think back to my uncle. I realize how much a football game for me has stopped being about good guys and bad guys. I also realize how much this shift, by making the game more about what it really is, increases my enjoyment. It helps me better appreciate the nuance of the game, and in what could seem a surprise, also more deeply feel the real intensity of the competition.

A specific concept within Creative Systems Theory—what it calls the Myth of the Individual—helps further fill out what is being asked of us. It puts what getting beyond thinking in ally and enemy terms requires in historical perspective. It also highlights this achievement's significance and its fundamental newness. The concept takes us well beyond how we tend to think in our time, but once understood, it is fundamentally important—and radical. And its implications can be readily expanded to capture what identity of the more collective sort today more generally is asking of us.

The Myth of the Individual alerts us to an essential recognition. The defining achievement of the Modern Age project is commonly thought of as a final realization of the individual as choice-maker. But what we have seen to this point has in fact remained fundamentally short of this result. To illustrate this recognition, I often highlight a couple of Modern Age assumptions. The first is the belief that modern democratic governance represents "government by the people"—in the sense of determination by individuals. The other is the belief with Romeo and Juliet–style romantic love that we have similarly realized love based on individual choice.

It is important to affirm that both modern representative government and romantic love have represented major steps forward. But it is just as important to recognize that in each case the result was not what we have thought it to be. In neither case have we witnessed individual identity in the Whole-Person, all-the-crayons-in-the-box sense that comes with Cultural Maturity's cognitive changes. In each case, identity was mythologized—based on one half of a polar dynamic.

Needed insights regarding governance start with the recognition that historically we have always elevated our leaders and made them more than just human. We have projected onto them much of our own authority. This kind of mythologizing is most obvious with times well past, when kings and god-kings provided unquestioned, even divine authority. But while today we tend to assume that we have left such dynamics behind us, in fact authority relationships with modern democratic governance have for the most part remained of a two-halves-make-a-whole, mythologized sort. Think of Kennedy in Camelot or Ronald Reagan as the kind father figure.

Modern romantic love, in that it took us beyond having determinations made by the family or a matchmaker, was more about choice than love had been historically. But in a similar way it remained based on idealization and projection. I, as a man, projected an idealized aspect of the archetypally feminine onto the woman, and the woman did the complement with an idealized archetypally masculine part of herself. Brave knight meets fair maiden. Again we see identity based on two-halves-make-a-whole assumptions.[1]

The focus with each of these examples is on individual identity of a personal sort, but we could make a related observation with regard to more collective identity. When collective identity requires enemies, in an analogous way it stops short of identity in any fully systemic sense. It remains a mythologized, two-halves-make-a-whole kind of identity. And this is the case equally when the enemy in question is another nation or a group with a contrasting political or social ideology.

The examples of watching football with my uncle and appreciating needed new steps in how we think about identity in spheres as different as governance and love in different ways bring us to the same place when it comes to the identity task that I've proposed defines the larger question when it comes to us-versus-them beliefs. Getting beyond the polarized assumptions of times past depends on learning to think about identity in more complete—more systemic—ways. It will require some kind of process at least similar to the cognitive reordering that I've described with the concept of Cultural Maturity.

Extended Reflections

I've promised that with each of the book's more topic-specific chapters I would include some observations that extend its conclusions additional steps into the future. I am not suggesting in doing this that we should be further along than we are—there is no benefit in trying to get ahead of ourselves. I am also very specifically not implying idealized outcomes. One of the things that distinguishes Cultural Maturity's picture of possibility from common interpretations of what may lie ahead is that it is about confronting predicted developmental tasks, not some

---

1   *Cultural Maturity: A Guidebook for the Future* provides more detailed examinations of both of these examples.

process of final realization. I include these further reflections only to highlight the significance of the direction of change I have described.

But important distinctions acknowledged, looking into the future with regard to where getting beyond us-versus-them assumptions might take us has some striking implications. A couple when it comes specifically to governance come immediately to mind. One is the possibility of governance that comes a step closer to being real "government by the people," in the sense of determination by people bringing the whole of themselves to the tasks of determination. If there is a single change that most defines how Creative Systems Theory frames a possible next chapter in the evolution of government and governance, it is this. In such a picture, Whole-Person leadership and Whole-Person followership have complementary significance. In Chapter Nine I will reflect on possible ways this might manifest.

The other implication relates to major ways that the boundaries of governmental determination might be expected to change in centuries ahead. We tend to take it for granted that we will have strongest collective identification with the nation-state. But this has not always been the case and it is unlikely to remain so in the same sense in the future. Likely we will see a picture that is more like nesting bowls—or more specifically, like overlapping nesting bowls. Identifying with nation-state boundaries will continue to have a place, but more so than today, many kinds of determinations will need to be made more globally. And the concept of Cultural Maturity predicts that we should find a related deepening of appreciation for how often determinations are best made regionally or locally.

Notice that thinking in terms of overlapping spheres of determination requires a more Whole-Person/Whole-System understanding of identity. Ally-versus-enemy thinking would pretty quickly make this more complex understanding of collective identity unworkable. It also requires that we hold such identity in more dynamic ways. We need to be able to identify with multiple, evolving, overlapping systems. Chapter Six's more specific look at boundaries will expand further on this more dynamic, multifaceted picture and what it asks of us.

This kind of far-off conjecture is arguably of greatest interest to futurists like myself. For our purposes with this book, it at least further highlights the importance of addressing polarization and the apparent regression that we have seen over recent decades. Depending on how we understand regression's cause and how persistent it proves to be, such backsliding makes the possibility of any further steps in how we think about government and governance more difficult to grasp. And certainly it makes it more difficult to realize. Of more immediate consequence, as the simplest of compromises between competing beliefs become impossible to reach, it threatens to undermine the functioning even of government as we have known it.[2]

---

2   Chapter Eleven in *Creative Systems Theory* includes a section on the future of government and governance that examines both of the implications I have described in more detail.

CHAPTER THREE

Climate Change—Risk Assessment, Foresight, and Responsibility

I first wrote about the possible dangers of climate change over thirty years ago. At the time, I could not have imagined that we would be so slow in taking these dangers seriously. And certainly I did not have any sense that climate change would become so contentious and polarizing. Today it is one of the issues where we can assume people have taken unquestioning positions before conversations even begin.

The climate change debate provides further illustration of how the fact of polarization has less to do with what we think than how we think. Climate change as an issue has no obvious sides—there is simply evidence to examine. Yet today we find the question met immediately with knee-jerk responses.

What we find with climate change also provides a good example of how making progress on any essential issue necessarily starts with asking the right question. The question with climate change as conventionally asked focuses on whether the science is definitive—whether science has proven that climate change is real and man-made. But that was not the question I was asking decades back when I concluded that climate change needed to be taken seriously. I knew that solid data would take time and even if we had more data, proof in this sense is not what science is about. The real question with climate change is not whether the science is right or wrong, but rather whether the risks as best we can know them are worth the gamble. On the basis of risk assessment, it was clear to me even at that time that the climate change question had in effect already been answered.

It is a kind of question that we confront more and more often in today's world as we face the need to make essential decisions in spite of limits to what we can know for sure. An excerpt from an article I wrote at that time highlights the relationship between limits to what we can often know and the important role that effective risk assessment necessarily plays in addressing so many of the future's most critical concerns. It also invites reflection with regard to how the contributions of the Right and Left might interplay with the climate change question.

> Climate change provides a prime example of what happens when people fail to think in terms of systemic risk. We see people making the accurate limits-related observation that we can't know with absolute certainty whether global climate change is real and then using it to justify not responding to the threat. I often ask people who resort to such logic what they think the odds are that human-caused warming of the planet is happening and could have dangerous consequences. I make them commit to a number. I then ask them how they would feel about their children playing Russian roulette. Few people are willing to claim that the odds of global warming being real and significant are less than Russian roulette's one in six. And the few who might maintain this claim have a hard time escaping the recognition that their conclusion has more to do with ideology than carefully considered evaluation.

To appreciate how the contributions of the Right versus those of the Left pertain to the climate change debate, it helps to think of the climate question as having two parts. There is the question of whether human-caused climate change is real. There is also the question of just what to do if it is. The need to think more systemically applies in each case, but in ways that have different consequences.

With the question of whether climate change is real, it would be easy to think from the article that I side wholly with the position of the political left. In terms of where I end up, that is essentially true. I see climate change as a major threat. The important distinction is that ideology is not how I arrive at my conclusion. I consider people on the political left who assume climate change is real while knowing very little about it to miss the point just as fundamentally as climate change deniers. Their ideological blinders are much less likely to cause immediate harm than the absolutist claims of the political right, but the basis for their conclusions is no closer to being systemic in a culturally mature sense.

As far as what should we do, including all the crayons in the systemic box becomes more clearly essential. There are multiple strategies we can apply for addressing climate change. Some are more societal, others more technical. With each kind of strategy, the Right and the Left each have insights to contribute. They are also often in denial about significant blindnesses.

With more societal interventions, we commonly encounter traps on both the Right and the Left. If the Right is willing to entertain the basic conclusion that human-caused climate change is real, it is still likely to think that we can get away with making changes slowly. In fact, the data that we have makes clear that we really don't have the luxury of taking our time. But the Left is vulnerable to an opposite kind of trap. If we make changes without carefully thinking them through, we could see the collapse of economies. And most likely it would be the economic conditions of people who are already the most vulnerable that would be affected first. Those of more ideological inclination on the Left are quick to assert that the development of more sustainable energy resources will boost economies—and I agree, at least in the long term. But I also think that the common assumption of the Left that a transition to renewable energy will happen rapidly and smoothly without collateral damage is naïve and more a reflection of polarized thinking than any kind of reasoned reflection.

Ideological blindnesses also present obstacles when it comes to more technical solutions. Again, they intrude from both the Right and the Left. From the Right, as the consequences of rising temperatures mount, we could see a strong push to apply simple technical fixes. An array of approaches that could artificially lower planetary temperatures are potentially available—from the seeding of clouds to reflect the sun's rays, to altering ocean acidity, to less radical methods that capture and store carbon. But most good scientists counsel caution when considering at least the more extreme of such approaches. At this point we have no way of knowing whether the results ultimately would be of more harm than benefit. And certain unintended consequences could well be catastrophic. It is possible that over time we may decide that some such methods are safe enough given the alternatives—at least as temporary measures. My point is simply that if we do eventually decide to make use of more technical interventions, we must do so from reasoned consideration, not out of reactions of a simple-answer, ideological sort.

From the Left, blindnesses of a more technical sort manifest in the requirement that interventions must pass tests of ideological purity. The Left tends to assume that certain approaches—such as solar, wind, and geothermal—are unquestionably good (even a bit holy). These methods are appropriately celebrated as essential parts of any solution. But again, if we are to recognize where there may be tradeoffs and apply approaches wisely, the basis for choosing a method can't simply be ideology. We also need to be sure that other approaches that might have potential benefit are not dismissed out of hand. In my book *Hope and the Future,* I described how I have gone back and forth through the years as far as nuclear power's appropriate role. At one point in my life

I spoke out strongly against nuclear power. More recently, I have become more comfortable thinking of it as part of a solution, at least for the short term.[1] I have been surprised to find people on the Left not only taking immediate issue with this suggestion, but in several instances rejecting the whole book because I had entertained it.

The role of hydropower in the Pacific Northwest where I live further illustrates the complexities of thinking through strategies. Few energy sources are cleaner than hydroelectric. But it is also the case that dams kill salmon and other migrating fish. In response, there are calls to demolish many existing dams. Is this a good idea? In certain circumstances the answer is definitely yes. But in the context of climate change we are left balancing two essential potential benefits. Again my point is not to argue for one approach over another, rather simply to emphasize the nuance we must bring to our choices if they are to best serve in the long term.

Effective decision-making in response to climate change will require a sophistication of perspective that few people at this point bring to the conversation. It will demand a complex array of difficult choices and an acceptance of the fact that the unexpected could intrude at any step along the way. The one thing we can know for sure is that positions based on easy-answer political allegiances can only get in the way. Key to the necessary maturity of engagement will be having everyone

---

[1] My initial objections concerned both safety and the fact that we have no adequate solution to nuclear waste. The risks with climate change alter the safety equation. And a think tank we did at the Institute for Creative Development that brought together some of the best scientists in the world to address the problem of nuclear waste has somewhat tempered my concerns there as well. We discussed how, while we don't have any long-term solutions for nuclear waste, we do have simple ways of storing it for a few hundred years. After that time we will likely have discovered better ways to deal with it, perhaps even ways to utilize it. At the very least, we will have answered the question of just how we can best address climate change.

affected in the room. Equally key will be everyone involved being open to having their assumptions challenged.

To get at just what the needed more encompassing perspective will require of us, we can again draw on the Parts Work analogy. The no to the Right is that denial in the face of science is no longer an option. The yes is that values of all sorts need to be considered in setting priorities. The no to the Left is that economic as well as environmental considerations ultimately need to be taken into account. The yes to the Left is the importance of making the confronting of climate change a very high priority in the decades ahead.

We can also again find guidance for what is being asked of us in the recognition that new kinds of skills and capacities will be needed. In particular, climate change highlights the importance of taking a more ultimate kind of responsibility. Confronting climate change effectively will require a newly encompassing responsibility for our larger human well-being—and, in the end, at least in some sense for life as a whole. And as I've implied in focusing on risk assessment and the inadequacy of past ways of thinking, it also includes a new, more direct kind of responsibility for the truths we draw on. We no longer get the ready, "parental" assumptions of times past.

Note that this completeness of responsibility also requires something else that is new, a degree of foresight that has rarely before been needed or possible. We have all had classes on history in school—classes on the past—but few people have had classes on the future. That we haven't had classes on the future could seem reasonable given that there is so little that we can really know about it—until we recognize that the future is where we will all eventually live and the one thing that we have the option of affecting.

Each of the other, more specific needed new skills and capacities that I have noted also come into play. The importance of acknowledging complexity and uncertainty essentially defines good risk assessment. And risk assessment directly confronts us with the fact of real limits—

to what we can know and also to what we can do, at least at all safely. Here I've put particular emphasis on how successful risk assessment requires the acknowledgement of the limits inherent to single-crayon-in-the-systemic-box, ideological assumptions of all sorts.

The importance of surrendering the need for final truths and focusing instead on the assessment of risk is relevant to all of the most important questions ahead for the species. It is directly pertinent, certainly, to the challenge we examined with the previous chapter. Good global decision-making when it comes to war and peace will require that we make an endless complexity of risk and possibility discernments. The need for effective risk assessment also clearly steps to the forefront with other concerns that have cataclysmic implications. We find it, for example, with the foresight needed to adequately prepare for future pandemics. With the COVID-19 scourge, we had adequate warning that something like it would happen eventually, but we failed at the foresight task. In the end, learning to better assess risk will be pertinent with each of the topics that we will confront in chapters ahead. With most of them the consequences for failing to adequately evaluate risk will not be so immediate or so dire, but whether our interest lies with addressing health care reform, abortion, immigration, bigotry, the historical battle between science and faith, or the question of how we best think about human advancement, the ability to assess risk will be essential.

The task, again, is not just to think new things, but to think in new ways. Efforts that attempt to balance the concerns of the Right and Left can be a start when it comes to risk assessment, but by themselves they are vulnerable to ending only in endless debate and watered-down versions of time-worn solutions. Effective risk assessment requires at least the beginnings of Integrative Meta-perspective. We must step beyond once-and-for-all truths of all kinds and think in ways that are more encompassing and complete.

A More Creative Kind of Responsibility

This chapter's more extended reflections turn to the more general question of how to make good choices when we lack the clear guideposts of times past. It might again appear to take us a bit far afield. But the question is pertinent not just here, but to reflections in each of the chapters ahead.

I've emphasized how decision-making in a culturally mature reality requires a new, more ultimate kind of responsibility. This new responsibility has both content aspects and process aspects. The content aspect includes getting the data right and determining the values on which we will base our choices.[2] The process aspect of the new responsibility brings us back to the key lessons of this chapter, how the truths we draw on require us to apply foresight as we are able, and also to be more comfortable making choices in a more complex and uncertain world in which limits play a necessary role.

In the end, these lessons apply not just to risk but also to possibility. To keep the language simple, we could say that decision-making of all sorts becomes necessarily more exploratory and experimental. We could also say more "creative." It is an aspect of the needed greater responsibility that I give particular attention to in my book *Creative Systems Theory*. The following paragraphs are adapted from it.

Culturally mature perspective highlights the fact that what constitutes right choice is often permeated by change and uncertainty. Cultural Maturity has as much to do with how we make choices as with just what we might choose—even if we choose wisely. This is not at all to simply reduce truth to process.[3] But

---

2   Chapters Eight and Nine in different ways address the values dimension of the needed new responsibility.

3   If we are to avoid traps in our thinking, it is important that we recognize that we can fail at culturally mature understanding just as readily by mak-

it is true that in a whole new sense content and process cease being wholly separate concerns.

A good place to see the process side of this more dynamic picture is with how culturally mature decision-making is often more exploratory and experimental than what it replaces. I often use exploratory metaphors in my therapy practice—to help people confront questions of basic life direction and also to address specific life choices (with regard to profession, relationships, where to live, values to hold). Such metaphors help people shape their lives in ways that best honor their unique identity and contribution. In a sense, such concerns have always been exploratory. But in the past, cultural dictates—for both good and ill—have dramatically restricted options.

For people of more rational bent, I might talk about such inquiry as akin to the best of scientific experiments. Well-done experiments engage the experimenter in a sequence of creative responsibilities. The first is responsibility for asking a good question, one worthy of the experimenter's time and focus. Next comes responsibility for crafting experiments and developing hypotheses that might shed new light on that question. Finally comes responsibility for obtaining the most accurate and useful results.

Making good choices in a well-lived life tends to be messier than this. But when external guideposts are limited, we necessarily engage in a similar kind of progression. We start by selecting a worthy creative starting point (if the question concerns work, selecting an endeavor that excites and could prove ful-

---

ing truth primarily about process. We often see this failing with more psychological and spiritual beliefs.

filling; if it concerns love, choosing someone for whom we feel caring and who could be good for us). And we experiment. We observe and we try things out. And we listen for what brings fulfillment. In the process, we learn about ourselves (and, with love, the other person). And we learn about the shapes that choices might take (how we might approach work, or how to engage love in ways that best reflect two people's unique natures and their growing connection).

When approaching life experimentally, we need to be exceedingly honest with regard to what works and what does not. Like good science, a creatively lived life is only in a limited way about getting the answers we want. With both, the most irresponsible thing one can do is alter data so as to better fit our hopes. The task is to seek out what is creatively true. It is through this that we make choices that are right, and choices that matter.

Science metaphors are likely to get blank stares—or worse—from people of more emotional or intuitive bent. But the metaphor of the artist's creative process works equally well. I might talk about how a composer writes a piece of music or how a painter applies his or her craft. The artist's first responsibility is to discover a worthy creative impulse—a possibility to which one is deeply drawn. Next comes trying out different ways to give that impulse expression. Lastly, there is the task of discerning what works and what does not. Artistic expression is about listening for what is beautiful and exploring different ways to make that beauty manifest. As with good science, eloquent artistry requires incorruptible self-honesty—fudging the results gets us nowhere. And in a similar sense, we cannot know ahead of time exactly where that honesty will lead.

People can object to such use of experimental/exploratory metaphors. For example, some can find them initially a bit heady, too analytical. This is particularly common if the topic is something like love. My response is that consciously engaging love (or life more generally) as a process does in fact require careful discernment—though something ultimately more than analytical discernment. Culturally mature decision-making requires bringing nuanced perspective to all kinds of questions for which simple being, faith, or subjective passion have been the more appropriate kind of engagement in times past.

In an opposite sort of objection, a person might claim that experimental imagery is just too imprecise—too "loosey-goosey." Again, using love as an example, a person might argue that it leaves out the most important ingredient in relationship—commitment. But, in fact, approaching love as a creative process in the end implies greater attention to commitment. Certainly, commitment can be one of the most powerful tools we have for making relationship's creative life possible and sustainable. More, the absence of clear guidelines in a culturally mature reality gives the articulation of commitment and the determination of its forms ever greater importance. Even if the commitment choices we make are very traditional, they need a deeper level of personal commitment to sustain them. What the exploratory metaphor adds to traditional notions of commitment is a better appreciation for how the rules for success in love—and the meaning of commitment—change when we no longer have the luxury of unquestioned cultural dictates.

Exploratory language can be applied just as usefully to decision-making tasks of a more collective sort. The broader question of how best to manage the often-contradictory potentials of modern invention provides an example that ties directly to the task with climate change. Because many of our most important advances, along with promising good, also present significant danger, responsible management will be critical. But responsibility in the sense of just doing the right thing can be of only limited help when much that is most important for us to know can't be known in advance. Evaluation may involve a great complexity of causal factors—and there is always the possibility of wild-card events. There is no way to be certain—except to those of dogmatic persuasion—just what doing the right thing entails.

Faced with such uncertainty, how do we best proceed? Some people reflexively call for extreme caution. Others may assert that free and open discovery is the only hope we have. And looming over choices is the question of whether responsibly managing human invention and its consequences is really even possible. The drive to be toolmakers may be simply unstoppable, impervious to self-reflection.

The perspective offered by an exploratory approach provides at least the beginnings of a way beyond what might seem an impasse. It suggests that management as we customarily think of it may not be the right word. In the end, we can't really manage invention any more than we can once and for all manage the results of scientific experimentation, the creation of a work of art, or the outcome of love—and we would not want to. But this lack of final control does not save us from responsibility. And certainly it does not save us from the need to make hard choices. When outcomes defy prediction, acting responsibly requires assessing risk as we are able, and if action is needed, acting decisively. In any such effort, keeping in mind that what we are engaged in is necessarily an experiment helps assure the right balance of humility and courage.

An exploratory framing of responsibility and choice also translates to the larger task of addressing our human future as a whole. Facing the future responsibly requires that we accept that what lies ahead necessarily defies final prediction. This more exploratory kind of responsibility demands more of us, but with Cultural Maturity's changes it becomes something we can be capable of. And increasingly we are seeing that it is the only kind that can work. We also increasingly recognize that when we consciously move beyond absolutist beliefs and think in more exploratory ways, not only do we make better headway, very often we find wholly unexpected solutions.

Today we are at best taking first baby steps in our ability to carry out such difficult shared decision-making. But we can be sure that our well-being will more and more depend on it. When we look back at ourselves in a hundred years, if we are at all successful at devising social structures and mechanisms for making such choices, we will surely regard these as some of our times' greatest achievements.[4]

Climate Change and the Long Term

Let's return more specifically to the climate change question. We reasonably ask how effective our climate change efforts are likely to be. There is also the related question of just what we are likely to see as a result of such efforts in the decades and centuries ahead. Depending on how we respond to the threat of climate change, I could imagine there being some very different long-term consequences.

A decidedly negative picture is certainly possible. Increasingly we are recognizing tipping-point dynamics that could dramatically multiply effects. And a negative picture is possible not just because of the direct consequences of climate change. If greenhouse gas levels continue to rise, we could well see the triggering of many other major dangers. We could witness a dramatic increase in the risk of conflict at a world scale highlighted in the previous chapter, major food shortages, acceleration of species extinctions, and further exacerbation of the gap between the world's haves and have-nots with a broader destabilization of world

---

[4]   Extended observations in Chapter Nine reflect briefly on what possible social structures and mechanisms might look like.

economies. Ultimately the greatest danger could lie with how climate change and its various consequences could amplify the regression and polarization we see today such that the more general greater maturity we need as a species becomes impossible to realize. Unfortunately, even if we could stop greenhouse gas emissions at current levels, the effects will still be considerable.

But that is not the only possibility. It is also possible that we could better wake up to these risks and start taking more decisive action. Many nations are now getting solidly on board with addressing climate change. And where nations have dropped the ball, states and business-es have often done much better. Cultural Maturity's changes would greatly facilitate further progress, but a simple recognition of the price we will pay for continuing to drag our feet could by itself be sufficient to more forcefully move things along.

If we can more effectively respond to the dangers, we could also witness a further benefit pertinent to this book's inquiry. The topic of climate change could prove to be an essential teacher for the more general maturity of understanding on which our future depends. With many of the other topics we will examine in this book, we could get away with denial and wishful thinking for quite a while without dire consequences. But as we saw in the previous chapter with the need to confront the dangers presented by today's readily available weapons of mass destruction, climate change puts the need to think more systemi-cally immediately before us. And failing to think in a more grown-up way about climate change could bring unfortunate consequences more quickly than most people assume. As I write these words, wildfires are raging all along the west coast of the U.S. and the smoke is so dense that people are warned not to even go outside. It is hard to ignore the fact that something of great importance is being asked of us.

CHAPTER FOUR

Health Care Reform and the Wisdom of Limits

I first wrote about the health care delivery dilemma even earlier than I did the importance of addressing climate change. In a similar way, initially I could not have guessed that it would produce the highly polarized responses that we witness today. Indeed, I assumed that it was a concern that most people would find rather boring. While radical new treatments understandably grab headlines, working out the details of health care delivery would seem more the province of hospital administrators and economic bean counters.

That health care reform might become so loaded an issue could seem even more perplexing given where the current version of the debate started. Earlier I noted how the model for much of the Affordable Care Act (Obamacare) was a Republican plan, the program Mitt Romney instituted in Massachusetts. Yet few concerns today more quickly result in advocates retreating to their respective corners.

Health care delivery makes a particularly good example of just how demanding the important new questions can be. As a physician as well as a futurist, it was clear to me decades back that if the health care delivery dilemma was not effectively addressed, the result could be an economic and social train wreck. Importantly, the health care delivery crisis is not just a U.S. crisis. The factors that make addressing it so challenging apply whatever a country's approach to health care. In time they will confront even the countries that now have the most enlightened of policies.

One of those needed new skills and capacities—the importance of a new maturity in our relationship with limits—provides language for articulating the larger question. I've described how the Modern Age narrative was heroic (or more precisely, heroic/romantic). Our task on confronting limits has been to defeat (or transcend) them. The health care delivery debate combines two concerns—access to care and cost containment—that when put together present us with limits that cannot be escaped. Most immediately they confront us with the reality of economic limits. And as I will get to shortly, ultimately, they confront us with an even more fundamental and easily disturbing kind of limit.

The larger question when framed in terms of economic limits becomes: "How do we address health care delivery in a way that acknowledges limits to what we can afford?" The need to address economic limits challenges the thinking of both the Right and the Left. As commonly articulated, the health care delivery debate pits free-market approaches against more centralized, government-directed strategies. People assume that choosing one economic approach or the other will provide a solution. In fact, we could make most any kind of approach work. But none of them can work unless we start by first acknowledging the fact of economic limits and their implications.

Health care expenditures today are spiraling uncontrollably—for everyone, whatever kind of system they employ—and there is no natural end in sight.

Advocates on each side tend to pin the problem on inefficiencies and excesses. They assume that if we just get the incentives right and set curbs against unreasonable profit-taking, all will be well. But while inefficiencies and excesses play some role in today's health care crisis, the most important factor is more basic. Spiraling costs are primarily a product of modern medicine's great success. Early innovations—like sterile technique and penicillin—were relatively cheap. More recent advances—sophisticated diagnostic procedures, exotic new medications, transplant surgeries, and more—are increasingly expensive and promise only to get more so.

We face a stark reality. Unless we are willing to spend an ever-expanding percentage of national resources on health care, we have no choice but to restrict health care spending. This circumstance puts before us a whole new order of ethical challenge. We need only look to extreme reactions that follow any suggestion that we might have to "ration" care to appreciate the newness of what is being asked of us. We've always rationed care, at least in the sense of withholding care from those who were not able to pay for it. And often, effective care has simply not been available. But what is being required today is different. If we are to stop spiraling costs, eventually we must consciously limit health care, and not just care that is of questionable value, but care that is of real benefit.

An exercise I've done with groups highlights the unsettling reality of what is being asked of us. I start by handing participants a list of ten patient profiles—including both information about patient's lives and information about their illnesses—along with a budget. I then send the group off to a room for two hours with instructions to decide how the money should be spent. The choices that the exercise requires of participants can be so emotionally and morally wrenching that people refuse to make them. But the exercise is not an abstraction. It presents the task we inescapably face if we are to effectively address health care limits.

Few people in the political sphere recognize the full implications of the health care delivery crisis. The Affordable Care Act addresses access to care, but in spite of its name, it does little of substance to confront health care costs. Calls for "Medicare for all" better address access, but in the end almost wholly ignore cost containment (while denying that they are doing so). Republicans now want their own plan, but they clearly have little appreciation for the complexities involved, certainly not the economic complexities. Eventually we must confront the fact of real limits.

The need to confront economic limits also highlights each of the other new skills and capacities I have touched on. Making health care choices with an acceptance of real limits to what we can afford demands a really quite ultimate kind of responsibility. And because there are no cut-and-dried rules for making such decisions, we necessarily face easily overwhelming complexities and uncertainties. And again, too, we confront the role of context. What addressing health care limits asks is going to be very different depending on when and where choices need to be made. Rarely, even with the best of thinking, will we have the luxury of one-size-fits-all prescriptions.

What is it that makes the task of confronting economic limits so much more demanding than people tend to assume? Simply the need to make agonizing choices would be enough of an explanation. And the fact that choices require this much of us certainly adds to the challenge. But there is more, and more of major consequence. At the least, not providing care when we have effective care to offer calls into question the heroic mythology that has defined modern medicine. And there is a further even more unsettling contributor. In the end, effectively confronting health care limits demands a new relationship to the most taboo of limits-related topics: our human mortality.

Medicine has always been about life-and-death decisions. But limiting care in the sense I'm suggesting involves consciously withholding care that might at least delay death's arrival. Add this recognition, and we get the needed even larger question: "What would it mean to approach health care in a way that acknowledges the importance of a new maturity in our relationship with death?"

It is important to appreciate how fundamentally this further question is new—and significant. Death represents life's ultimate limit to what we can know and control. Always before in our history, cultural belief has served to keep death's full significance at arm's length. Increasingly we are having to confront that this kind of distancing has stopped being an option. Effectively confronting health care limits could make addressing other death-related issues such as abortion, assisted suicide, or capital punishment seem like child's play. Remember early on with the introduction of the Affordable Care Act how effective the claim that health care delivery changes might result in "death panels for grandma" was in stopping conversation in its tracks.

What exactly would good political leadership with regard to the health care delivery challenge look like? Certainly it would include some of what we find with the best of current efforts at health care reform. It would emphasize better covering the uninsured, giving greater attention to preventive care, addressing drug costs, and more extensive application of evidence-based medicine. But politicians who want to provide real leadership would also reopen the conversation in a way that better acknowledges the fact of real economic limits. And over time, leadership must go further. It must help people in coming to better appreciate the importance of a greater maturity in our relationship to death.

In the end, needed leadership must ultimately come from all of us. People today tend to celebrate every new, more expensive medical advance at the same time that care becomes increasingly unaffordable, both for individuals and for society. As citizens, we must be clear that this is not sustainable—and ultimately really not sane. And, like it or not, political leadership is one of the last places where we are likely to find an appreciation for a greater maturity in our relationship to death. That can happen best through our everyday conversations.

If we look to health care settings, in fact we already see changes when it comes to this more ultimate challenge—only first steps, but ones that are significant. For example, we witness growing recognition of the importance of end-of-life conversations between patients and doctors. The role of quality hospice care is increasingly appreciated. And states are beginning to pass legislation that supports doctor-assisted suicide. None of this would happen without broader societal changes in how we view death and its implications.

It is important to appreciate how more directly confronting health care limits, even just economic limits, could have effects well beyond the obvious. It could contribute not just to rethinking access to care, but also to increasingly mature and empowered insights about what it takes to be healthy, what it means to heal, and more broadly, about the requirements of a healthy society. Start addressing health care limits and pretty soon we begin examining questions that expand the health care picture dramatically. We might ask, for example, whether access to good nutrition should be emphasized as part of prevention. And if yes, then what about cleaning up toxic chemicals in the environment? And if that too is part of health care's larger picture, what about lack of housing...and today's larger challenge of bringing greater maturity to how we understand and act? That might seem to stretch the systemic interpretation too far. But for today, isn't that just what the doctor ordered—a fresh, really big-picture look at the whole health care endeavor?

The questions presented by the health care delivery crisis are not just harder than we tend to recognize, arguably they are harder than we have been capable of recognizing up to this point in our development as a species. But they are also the questions that we have to ask. In the end, confronting health care limits should result not just in care that we can afford, but also in care that is more complete, that better addresses the whole of who we are as individuals and as societies. And while getting there will ask a lot of us, we can also think of it simply as bringing the needed "new common sense" to the health care sphere.

Death's Challenge to Understanding

In my book *Rethinking How We Think*, I touch on a good way to expand on these reflections. I examine how the idea of a needed new maturity to death challenges understanding more broadly. I've proposed that cultural belief has always before in history served to keep death's full significance at arm's length. We benefit from looking at this statement more closely drawing on reflections from the earlier book. This is not a kind of claim that should be made without evidence. It is also a recognition that provides further insights into how Cultural Maturity's changes alter thinking more generally.

A person could legitimately argue that looking more squarely at death is nothing new—just new for medicine. For example, one might claim that religion is a sphere that long ago made its peace with death. Funerals most commonly take place in churches. And religious settings are where we are most likely to encounter conversations about our mortality and find solace in the face of death. Indeed, if we go back far enough, we often find death-related imagery intimately tied to spiritual experience. Burial mounds were places of worship for the ancient Celts, and writings such as the Tibetan Book of the Dead have served as guides to spiritual realization.

But this argument misses how religion has always before also distanced us from death's full significance. By providing unquestioned explanation for what happens after death, religion has also served to protect us from death as experience.

Putting how religion has conceived of death in historical perspective supports this conclusion. It also helps us appreciate how our relationship to death has changed before. Each stage in the evolution of spiritual/religious understanding has provided us with a somewhat different picture of what happens after we die. Each of these pictures, in a way consistent with the realities of that cultural stage, offered a sense of order and gave us a way to reconcile with death. But each also, in the end, protected us from the fact of death.

In tribal times, death was thought of as allowing us to rejoin nature and our ancestors in a parallel world. Later, with the early rise of civilizations and more polytheistic sensibilities, we commonly encounter belief in reincarnation, with death bringing a return to the present in some new form. With the emergence of monotheism, we came to think of death as providing entry into a now separate world—depending on our life choices, of either a heavenly or hellish sort. With the more liberal monotheism of Modern Age times, we tend most often to think of that separate world as simply a better and happier place.

Along with offering solace in death, religion continues to protect us from death's easily overwhelming implications. While different modern religions vary in the degree that they emphasize this protective function, it is never totally absent. I remember at my mother's funeral how the minister seemed ultimately more concerned with reassuring everyone that my mother was now with God (and that everything was thus right and as it should be) than with my mother as a person. It became quickly clear to me that this was really not the place to be if I wished to grieve my mother's passing with the depth that had come to feel important to me.

Drawing on religion's history in this way leaves us with a fascinating question: How might religion change if it underwent similar changes to those I've proposed will be necessary for medicine? The answer could not help but be transforming.[1]

In asking how a new, more mature relationship with death might alter religion, it is only fair that we ask the same question of science. A person might imagine that in challenging religion's protective role I am instead siding with science's conclusion—that death is just death, the end of us. But death's challenge to science is ultimately just as basic. At the very least we have to acknowledge that science's conclusion is ulti-

---

[1]   It is a question that I take on directly in *Creative Systems Theory*. Chapter Nine in this book provides a few hints at an answer.

mately just as much an "article of faith." Scientists share with theologians the fact that neither can describe death from personal experience.

In addition, the same cognitive reordering that invites us to reflect anew on the future of religion takes death's challenge to science an important step further. Culturally mature perspective makes clear that while modern science's view of the world has contributed powerfully, the kind of "objectivity" that science relies on remains partial.[2] The aspects of experience that the traditional scientific worldview leaves out would be expected to make scientific interpretation especially unhelpful when it comes to making sense of death. In the end, the death question confronts science (at least science of the narrow scientism[3] sort) as fundamentally as it does religion, and the implications could be just as transformative.[4]

Basic observations that have been key to this book's argument support death's challenge to the traditional thinking of both religion and science in a more conceptual way. I've described how any time we find beliefs that are commonly framed in terms of polar opposites, something important is likely missing in each formulation. And it is not just that each polar formulation captures only part of a larger, more systemic picture. We discover that all along neither side has been asking the important larger question. We appropriately expect this to be the case with religion and science when it comes to the question of death.[5]

There are also other spheres where the possibility of a greater maturity in our relationship to death is pertinent. With some, the connec-

---

[2]   Chapter Nine in this book examines specific ways in which the worldview of classical science remains limited. Chapter Ten addresses more conceptually why this might be the case.

[3]   Scientism assumes that the kinds of observations that come with the application of the scientific method explain everything.

[4]   Again, see *Creative Systems Theory*.

[5]   In the next chapter, I will propose that the question of life is just as ultimately perplexing, and just as important to address if we are to make good choices going forward.

tion is obvious and changes are already underway. For example, I don't think we would see today's questioning of capital punishment—and the willingness to entertain more nuanced decisions about where it might be appropriate—without these changes. But in addition, there are domains where these changes are relevant but where death's role is not so explicit. I think most immediately of the media, both serious media—such as news media—and media of a more entertainment sort.

While many of the most important media-related changes will likely be a long time in coming, they could ultimately be some of the most significant. Our ambivalent feelings toward death—at once attraction and repulsion—are key to much of modern media's success. News of an "if it bleeds, it leads" sort commonly garners the greater portion of airtime; it is rare to find television intended for adults that doesn't involve at least one shooting (and more often many more); and killing—and the possibility of being killed—is pretty much what "action" movies and most popular video games are about. Modern media draws us in by creating a narrative tension between life and death.

But if what I have described for other spheres is accurate, this narrative tension is born of an increasingly outmoded and unhelpful relationship with death. It is based on a polarized and mythologized picture that makes death if not evil, certainly our adversary. I find it fascinating to reflect on how the kind of "growing up" in how we view death that the concept of Cultural Maturity predicts might, in the long term, alter media—of all sorts. Because the media could in potential provide needed leadership with regard to broader cultural changes, we should demand it.

The place where a new, more mature relationship with death may have its most significant effect is even less immediately obvious. I've described the core crisis of our time as a Crisis of Purpose. As understandings of significance tied to culture's past parental role fail us (whether it be the American Dream or our favorite religious or political ideology), we are being called on to address what matters in more conscious and encompassing ways. Coming face to face with mortality in our individual lives teaches us about what most matters to us as individuals—death is a personal life's most pointed teacher of meaning, and ultimately of wisdom. As we learn to engage death collectively with a new maturity, it is reasonable to think that this engagement should help us in a similar way to more deeply confront what most ultimately matters to us more broadly—as humans.

Why is looking directly at death so difficult that historically it has been essentially impossible? Obviously, death confronts us with the fact that life as we know it ends—not a comfortable recognition. But as I observed in introducing these reflections, death also confronts us with what is an even more final and disturbing limit. It confronts us with limits to what is possible to control and understand. Before now, facing this particularly absolute kind of limit would not have been compatible with sanity.

To fully grasp why we would want to do so even with Cultural Maturity's changes, we need to appreciate a further manifestation of the apparent paradox that I noted earlier. We encounter it any time we address limits more systemically—as with personal maturity in our individual development and in a more encompassing sense with Cultural Maturity. Lacking mature perspective, we experience real limits as problems, at best as adversaries to be defeated, at worst as evil. With Cultural Maturity's cognitive changes, we better see how inviolable limits are nothing exceptional. They are just part of how reality works—an essential aspect of what is. Understood in this way, the importance of new maturity in our relationship with death becomes straightforward, even simple, just part of the needed new common sense.

This recognition at least helps us grasp how acknowledging limits might have benefits. It suggests that acknowledging limits might let us perceive more clearly. And there is more. In the end, acknowledging real limits, rather than limiting us, does the opposite. By helping us better appreciate life's complexities and nuances, it frees us to better see options, to recognize what in fact is possible. As far as the needed new maturity in relationship with death, nothing is more inescapable and obvious than the fact that we die. And at the same time, directly confronting this simple fact—both within specific domains and more broadly—should prove to be one of our most important teachers going forward.

Broader Implications and Timelines

A couple of questions are reasonable to ask in wrapping up. The first concerns how the need to address health care limits might interplay with other aspects of today's challenges. We also appropriately ask just how quickly we should expect to see the kind of changes I've described.

As far as more encompassing effects, it is possible, as I described with climate change, that the primary contribution—at least in the short term—will not be positive. I've emphasized how effectively addressing health care limits will be more fundamentally demanding than most anyone at this point recognizes. The health care delivery crisis could contribute significantly to today's sense of overwhelm and the regression that easily results.

But as we also saw with the climate change challenge, it is possible too that the need to address health care limits could serve in important ways to support the broader realization of culturally mature capacities. Again, while the challenge is considerable, there is really no way to escape it. The health care delivery crisis could well serve as a particularly important force toward helping us grasp the importance of Cultural Maturity's larger changes. Again, it is up to us.

With regard to timeframes, given that acknowledging health care limits stretches us as deeply as it does, such changes could take longer than certainly I would hope. The confrontation with death that comes with restricting care is particularly direct—and often agonizing. But it is also the case with health care limits, even more so than what we saw with climate change, that consequences confront us today. Cultural Maturity–related change is never just some luxury—a nice option that we can get to when it might be convenient. But with health care limits, it should not be long before escalating costs stop us in our tracks. Changes thus could happen more quickly than we might imagine.

What I can say confidently is that however rapidly we see changes, the willingness of the health care world to move beyond our Modern Age limits-denying narrative should be increasingly critical to health care being a life-affirming endeavor in the decades and centuries ahead. I am also comfortable with the assertion that each step we make in this regard will function to support the more systemic and mature—complex and wise—understandings that the future more generally requires.

CHAPTER FIVE

Abortion—Looking Squarely at the Question of Life

Abortion is another issue where we find polarization becoming only more extreme. Certainly opinion has come to more clearly divide along party lines. For example, in the 1970s Republican President Gerald Ford opposed *Roe v. Wade*,[1] while both First Lady Betty Ford and Ford's vice president Nelson Rockefeller were abortion-rights supporters. Today, we confront conflicting views that might seem beyond reconciliation. Certainly in practice people rarely succeed in finding common ground. But precisely because the abortion question so quickly splits people into opposing camps, it warrants our attention.

We encountered what is likely the main reason behind such extreme disparity of belief in the previous chapter. There I proposed that the health care debate in the end becomes so deeply contentious because it brings us face to face with life's ultimate limit—the fact that we die. More specifically, it requires that we make conscious choices in the face of death. Abortion in a related way confronts us with questions of life and death. And whatever our position, in the end, it similarly requires that we make life-and-death–related choices.

---

1   The case that made abortion legal in the United States.

Consulting work I did a few years back with a social services organization provides a way in. Abortion had become a hot-button issue in the organization, and contentious feelings were getting in the way of people working together effectively. I've mentioned that I often use the same general kind of approach that I apply with Parts Work with groups. I am particularly likely to do so with groups that are experiencing internal conflicts or where a group is dealing with controversial issues.

When working in this way, I start by having individuals or small subgroups represent the competing voices. A second group, sitting separate from them, assumes the role of the Whole-Person/Whole-System chair. People in this second group are given a sequence of tasks. First they engage the advocate groups in conversation to clarify the divergent positions. They then converse among themselves and seek to find larger ways of thinking. And finally, they attempt to articulate conclusions and describe how these larger ways of understanding might translate into right and timely action.

I began in working with the organization by separating out two small groups to speak for the pro-life and pro-choice positions. (To make things more interesting, I switched the groups so that people in each group had to argue for a position opposite to what they actually believed. I then had people who actually held those positions be consultants to help the advocates effectively make their arguments.) The rest of the participants—those tasked with finding larger perspective— sat in a circle outside the advocate groups.

To start the process, the two small groups spoke in turn (with the consultants coaching so the advocates didn't miss important points). The main arguments were those we commonly hear. The pro-life group argued that abortion was murder. The pro-choice group countered that the decision should be in the hands of the woman (or the woman and her doctor).

Next I invited people in the outer circle to ask curiosity questions. Initially, their task was simply to clarify positions (the process allows no debate at this point). While this helped fill out understanding, it failed to provide much that altered the conversation. The positions of the two groups continued to appear mutually exclusive.

The people in the outer circle then took on the further task of attempting to engage the issue of abortion more systemically. Initially I had them discuss quietly in pairs. And with time I had them share together and do their best to articulate their conclusions. While the outer group's efforts didn't provide final answers, their reflections did gradually move the conversation from a debate about right and wrong to interactions that acknowledged legitimate feelings on both sides.

Several contributions proved particularly useful in this regard. A man who leaned more pro-choice offered that he found it impossible to escape that abortion was in fact a kind of killing—that at the least it was the ending of a potential life. He briefly apologized to his pro-choice colleagues that they might not be happy with his conclusion. But he quickly went on to suggest that denying this reality was only hiding from the real question and made real conversation impossible. And in the end, it simply left out what he felt was an essential fact.

A woman who leaned more pro-life at first also apologized, observing that while what she had to offer had helped her, others might find it too philosophical. She described how she had found herself questioning whether death was the right way to think about the opposite of life. She struggled to find words that might express a better way of thinking about it. Eventually she proposed that maybe instead of being pro-life in a literal sense, people needed to think instead in terms of what most ultimately honored life. And while she wasn't quite sure what she meant, she also offered that being sure that life endured might not be the only way to do so. Several of her colleagues countered that such semantics accomplished nothing—that death could not be consistent with life—but the observation did invite people to begin to stretch their assumptions.

Conversations continued on for about an hour, going back and forth between the two advocacy groups and the people tasked with finding a larger picture. Rarely was there full agreement, but the stated goal—of generating greater mutual respect—was gradually achieved. People were able to get to the place where productive conversation at least became possible.

Reframing the Question

I often use the abortion debate to illustrate a principle that proves important most any time polarized belief manifests in quandaries of a specifically moral sort. We tend to assume that moral quandaries require us to choose between good and evil. But if a question is rightly framed in good-versus-evil terms, it is really not a quandary. It then tends to be obvious what we need to do. Rather, moral quandaries juxtapose competing goods. Clearly this is the case with the abortion debate. It pits the sanctity of life against a woman's right to choose. Each is clearly a good—and an important kind of good.

This principle can provide a start with reframing the abortion debate. But people aren't used to thinking in terms of competing goods. And the task is compounded by a further circumstance that we commonly find with thorny issues. Each position advocates for a very different kind of good. Caught with such apples-and-oranges considerations, we confront major difficulties not just because different people may value one good as opposed to the other. Because we are dealing with wholly different concerns, there is no way we can meet half-way even if we were inclined to do so.

Our approach with this book suggests a way to at least move a step closer, though it can only help us if a person is ready for this level of reflection. With each of the previous topic-specific chapters, we've seen the power of trying to articulate a larger question. It is reasonable to ask what the larger question might be with the abortion debate.

Traditionally, with the abortion debate, the defining question concerns when life begins. Those of more conservative bent will claim it begins at conception—or at least at the time of a first fetal heartbeat. Those of more liberal inclination will tend to answer the question in terms of viability. But the "when does life begin" question proves much less helpful than we might imagine. Because each answer is in its own way legitimate, there is no clear justification for choosing one over the other. The viability answer also confronts the fact that as medical science has improved, this measure has become a moving target.

There is in fact a larger question that can at least begin to take us forward. We can hear hints of it in the responses of each of the outer-circle contributors in the group Parts Work example. The better question asks what choices are most ultimately life-affirming, in the sense specifically of supporting life as something we experience as meaningful. This kind of determination is less objective. It is not something that we can discern at a safe arm's length. And people can continue to disagree in how they answer it. But arguably it gets more directly at what is important.

Framing the question in this way at least begins to provide a basis for conversation. Note that at the same time it supports and fundamentally challenges the positions of both the Right and Left (in Parts Work terms, presents both yeses and nos for each side). For the Right it affirms that the fact of life is a good (the yes). But at once it requires acknowledging both that when life begins is open for debate and that existence is not the only variable when it comes to a meaningful life (the no). For the Left it supports the importance of a woman's right to choose (the yes in doing Parts Work). But at the same time it requires the Left to acknowledge that abortion does in fact end a possible life (the complementary Parts Work no).

This more personal kind of framing offers something important that is not an option with more absolutist answers—the possibility of change, and even surprises. A physician friend recently told me about a group she had led for women who had had abortions earlier in their lives. She recounted the story of one woman who, at the time of her abortion in her twenties, had viewed abortion primarily as a freedom to be exercised. Only later did the woman come to feel deep emotional pain and the experience of real loss. Looking back, the woman questioned if she had made the right choice. For another woman, the surprise was of an almost opposite sort. The choice to have an abortion for her had been agonizing. It ran counter to her religious beliefs and her own cherishing of life. But reflecting back, she realized that proceeding with it had been one of the most important—and courageous—acts of her life.

As we've seen with other issues, just identifying a more systemic way of thinking doesn't provide an answer that will be acceptable for everyone. Few people will find this way of framing the abortion question wholly satisfying. The main reason is the explanation that I offered earlier for why the abortion issue is so fraught. Abortion brings us face to face with death. But we can also think of the reason in terms of any of the needed new skills and capacities I've noted. Certainly framing the abortion question more systemically confers new responsibility, and of the ultimate sort I've pointed toward. It makes us newly responsible not just for choosing correctly, but for the truths on which we base our choices. With culturally mature perspective, we see that accepting this greater responsibility becomes part of what it means to be moral in our time. But taking this level of responsibility in the truths we draw on is not something we are used to doing.

It is also the case that we can't really approach the abortion question more systemically without confronting the need for each of the more specific new skills and capacities I have noted. We need to accept the fact that choices are complex. And inevitably we need to acknowledge that the act of choosing involves real uncertainty. Like it or not, too, we find real limits, at least with regard to the usefulness of more ideological ways of thinking, but also ultimately to what anyone can know for sure. We also again confront the fact of truth's contextual relativity. How we might answer the abortion question is going to be influenced by the degree to which we can tolerate a more systemic picture and manifest these new skills and capacities. It can also be influenced by personality style. And how abortion is viewed can also be very different depending on life circumstances, such as religious background.[2]

The Question of Life

This chapter's more extended reflections take systemic perspective even further. This is further than many people will find useful. And as I will come back to, specifically with regard to abortion they present a picture that could be used equally well to argue for each of the traditional positions. But they are at least intriguing with regard to how larger ways of thinking can add to understanding.

I've described the difficulty of framing the abortion question in terms of when life begins. It turns out that the problem is ultimately more fundamental than just that the answer is open to debate. It has to do with the very nature of life. In fact, the "what is life" question baf-

---

[2]   Life circumstances also include locale. Today, abortion is available on request (with certain restrictions) in North America, most of Europe and Scandinavia, Russia, China, and Australia. It is allowed only to preserve health or to save the woman's life in the larger portion of South and Central America and Africa. And in a small number of countries, mostly in Africa and the Middle East, it is banned altogether. How we think about abortion will also be relative not just with regard to where we live, but also to when. Ireland legalized abortion only in 2018. And today how we think about abortion remains very much in flux. *Roe v. Wade* was argued nearly 50 years ago, and arguably it leapt ahead of the thinking of the ma-

fles even the best of scientists. Commonly they just hand it to a philosopher—who in the end can do no better.

Biologist and systems theorist Gregory Bateson was fond of beginning biology classes by placing a live crab at the front of the room and then asking students how they knew it was alive. He would then exit the room and leave them to ponder. On his return, he'd respond to each student's answer by describing something that is not alive that also exhibits that characteristic. "It moves." Certainly cars move. "It grows and reproduces." Crystals also grow and reproduce. And so on. The students were left with the easily startling recognition that there may be no ready answer to the question that most defines biology—and in an important sense most defines themselves.

But there is a way of responding to the "what is life" question that comes close to providing an answer. Biologist Lynn Margulis has put it this way: "Life is matter that chooses."[3] Creative Systems Theory reaches a related conclusion if we use the word "choose" most generally. Life at its most basic at least chooses in the sense of tropism—a paramecium moves toward its food source and away from environments it would find aversive. Higher life forms make more complex kinds of choices. And some, like ourselves, choose more consciously.[4]

Might answering the "what is life" question in this way be pertinent to the abortion question? In attempting to address abortion more systemically, I have used the phrase "life-affirming" as a metaphorical

---

jority of people in the U.S. at the time. Since then, several states have chipped away at its freedoms, and it could still be overturned.

[3]   As recounted by Steve McIntosh in his book *Developmental Politics* (Paragon House, 2020).

[4]   Notice that this way of thinking requires us to get beyond the Modern Age assumption that living things are best thought of as collections of mechanistic reflexes. Today we are better appreciating how living systems of all sorts are more richly complex in their functioning than we have assumed in times past. In Chapter Ten, I will describe how this more systemic picture also has radical implications for how we understand choice in human systems.

pointer. But the phrase only begins to bridge the divide. Framing life itself more systemically at least helps do so more conceptually. Life and choice then stop in the same sense being separate concepts. Arguably being pro-life then becomes about siding with choice in the largest sense. And being pro-choice becomes about choosing in ways that ultimately honor life.

Such abstract pondering is not going to be of great help for most people when it comes to the abortion question. These observations go well beyond how most people are interested in thinking. And a person could legitimately conclude that any pertinence to the abortion question is just wordplay. Of more immediate importance, these reflections could in fact be used to support traditional positions as easily as they could to support getting beyond them. On the pro-choice side, they make human life not quite so unique and increase our appreciation for the profundity of choice. And on the pro-life side, just as appropriately, they could be seen as highlighting the profundity of life and the need to protect it at all costs. The pertinent recognition for our purposes may be simply how strikingly our understanding of reality can change when we are willing to look afresh at basic questions.[5]

Culturally mature understanding, however we frame it, doesn't alter the fact that people can legitimately arrive at very different answers when it comes to the abortion question. What bringing more systemic perspective to the abortion debate does perhaps do is make it possible to think in more generous ways. As I described with the group Parts Work example, even making a start in this direction offers that mutual respect and meaningful conversation might then more often be options.

---

[5]   In Chapter Ten, I will touch on how this kind of larger systemic picture can help us address even more fundamental philosophical quandaries such as the apparent contradiction between free will and determinism.

CHAPTER SIX

What the Immigration Debate Can Teach Us About Boundaries, Interrelationships, and Collective Identity

Immigration policy is another area where conversation today increasingly becomes contentious and polarized. At the populist extremes, assertions can be made that are really quite ludicrous. On the extreme Right we find an ethno-nationalism that essentially objects to immigration of any sort—"build that wall." On the extreme Left we encounter views that can come close to suggesting that having borders at all is morally wrong.

Often the result is not just confusion, but the perpetration of real harm—from both sides. From the Right, shortsighted exclusionist policies do damage to those who might seek to immigrate. Such policies also often do harm to countries that might be rewarded by the kinds of contributions immigrant populations have traditionally made to their new homes. From the Left we can find stances that can get in the way of thinking about border policy with the complexity needed for policy that ultimately benefits us. We also find those who assert that borders are important being reflexively labeled as racist. While bigotry can play a role when borders are emphasized, with the best of such views that is not the case.

This chapter won't concern itself with the specifics of immigration policy—that is beyond our scope and also beyond my expertise. Rather, our interest lies with the values and ways of understanding needed to produce the best policy decisions. Whatever kind of policy might be most appropriate in a particular situation, the basic observation that we need to bring greater sophistication to how we make immigration-related determinations is valid, and important.

As a way in, let me share an experience that has prompted me to think more deeply about the immigration question. Several years back, a valued colleague in England contacted me after reading an article I had written on immigration policy. He angrily challenged me that the article had an unacknowledged liberal bias. While historically he had been liberal in his views, he had been a supporter of Great Britain separating from the European Union. A main reason was that he felt the European Union had been unwilling to limit immigration in ways necessary for the health of the country. The fact that he had often felt denigrated and misunderstood for his position was part of what had motivated him to get in touch.

It was fascinating to compare our experiences. Immigration is central to the American story. We are a country of immigrants. And the influence of immigration in my home state of Washington has been almost wholly positive. That doesn't mean we haven't had controversy, but we would not have had a thriving apple industry in the state, or more recently a vital high-tech industry, if it were not for immigration (with much of it historically illegal). In contrast, my colleague lived in a part of London that had become largely immigrant. It felt to him that too often new immigrants were antagonistic to their new home—and, at the extreme, interested in doing harm to it. I don't think it is appropriate to assume that the job of newcomers is simply to assimilate—immigrants have always brought with them new colors and flavors of experience and transformed their new homelands in the process. But my colleague is an extremely intelligent and open-minded person and far from a bigot. I could understand how he might conclude, given current world circumstances, that the right response would be to revisit existing immigration policies.

Our conversation prompted me to think more complexly than I had previously about the immigration question, in particular to better appreciate the importance of being attentive to context. It also alerted me to how the immigration debate was another concern where a willingness to ask a larger kind of question and bring culturally mature perspective to bear would be important. As with the abortion debate, with immigration we encounter competing goods—in this case, protection and tradition on one hand, and freedom and opportunity on the other. The needed larger question once more comes back to the choices that will be most ultimately life-affirming. But here it concerns how we best support the life/vitality of social systems and nations—and in particular the role of boundaries in doing so.

I find four recognitions key if we are to get beyond polarized debate and address immigration in terms of this more encompassing question. None of them is ultimately complicated, but each requires more systemic perspective if it is to be effectively applied, or even fully grasped.

First, we need to think more consciously about immigration policies. The need to make immigration-related determinations has always been part of having borders. But in times past, basic policy assumptions were closely tied to culture's parental authority and absolutist cultural truths. Answering immigration questions wisely is another part of our new shared responsibility.

Second, we need to conceive of borders more complexly and dynamically. I often draw on the metaphor of a cell to get at what more is required. Cells are alive because they have boundaries—the cell membrane. Without a cell membrane, the cell would die. But to complete this recognition—and the metaphor—we also need to appreciate that it is just as much the case that the cell will die if the membrane is only a wall. We need to include a critical additional property. Cell membranes are "semi-permeable." Cells are most vital when the balance between the cell membrane's permeabilities and impermeabilities is just right. Similarly, societies are most vital and creative when the balance between boundary yeses and nos is determined correctly.

The third recognition is illustrated by the conversation with my English colleague. The right kind of border policy may be very different depending on the context. If we are to make good border policy, we must learn both to better tease apart how different contexts are different and to more effectively understand how various contexts may call for different kinds of policies.

A fourth kind of recognition is also important if boundary-related conversations are to be productive. Different people, by virtue of their makeup, are going to be more attuned to the permeability or impermeability aspects of any kind of boundary. People who think of themselves as liberals are most likely to identify with the permeability aspect of semi-permeability. "Openness" is an important value. People who think of themselves as conservative are most likely to identify with the exclusionary aspect of semi-permeability. They find particular importance in safety and in bonds with family and community. While they also value openness, it is openness within those bonds that is important to them. Such openness requires vigilance with regard to just who gets let in. If our border-related debates are to be at all civil—and certainly if they are to result in effective policy—we need to appreciate how the positions of each side reflect an important aspect of needed understanding.[1]

It is important to fully grasp the newness of what these recognitions ask of us. Our now familiar needed new skills and capacities pro-

---

[1] *Creative Systems Theory's* presentation of the Creative Systems Personality Typology provides a more detailed and differentiated picture of how various people will predictably embody these ultimately complementary values.

vide perspective. Certainly, being this conscious and responsible in how we think about borders is new. So too is thinking in ways that are this multifaceted and dynamic—that require, as we've seen with other topics, that we be more comfortable with complexity and uncertainty. Again, we also in a new way encounter limits, certainly to ways of thinking that make immigration only negative or positive. And again, too, we aren't accustomed to reflecting this deeply on context. That includes how what is true in one situation can be so different from what is true in another. It also includes being attentive to differences in viewpoint, and in particular, ways that such differences can benefit us.

We can turn to our Parts Work metaphor to further highlight what is new. The no to the Right is that immigrants need not be a threat. The yes is that if immigration is to add to our collective lives, we cannot shy away from the importance of having strong borders. The no to the Left is that ignoring distinctions that need to be made only denies an essential kind of responsibility. The yes to the Left is that when we accept the importance of this responsibility, immigration can be a powerfully positive force. Author and columnist Thomas Friedman has put it succinctly in speaking of the need for high walls with a big gate.[2]

Bringing Historical Perspective to the Immigration Debate

We can expand our understanding of what the immigration question asks of us by turning to the "when" aspect of context. A very quick, big-picture look at how border relationships between large cultural systems have evolved provides valuable further perspective. Of particular importance for these reflections, it helps us better understand how Cultural Maturity's changes alter our relationship to borders—and more specifically, how we think about immigration.[3]

---

[2]   From an October 2020 article in *The New York Times*.
[3]   These observations reflect Creative Systems Theory's developmental framework. See *Creative Systems Theory*.

In tribal times, we didn't need to give borders much thought. It is not that boundaries weren't important—indeed, quite the opposite. But to a degree that can be hard to grasp from our Modern Age vantage, tribal groups often lived in separate realities. We see evidence of this in how even groups that have lived in close proximity frequently have wholly different languages. For example, in modern Papua New Guinea, a place where tribal bonds are often still strong, we find over two hundred separate languages.

From the early rise of civilizations through the Middle Ages, we gradually became more directly concerned with boundaries. Increasingly we ventured beyond our borders, often for trade, but also for conquest. This meant sometimes letting boundaries down. But it also became increasingly important that boundaries when needed could be made in ways that were "hard and fast." Relationships between cultural systems came to be defined primarily in terms of power and dominion. Castle walls and impenetrable armor provide symbols for this more conscious relationship to boundary.

Western culture's Modern Age brought further extension beyond past bounds. We witnessed the Age of Exploration and later, with the Industrial Age, even greater commerce between the world's peoples. Relationships between cultural systems gradually became based more on economic competition and material advantage. As interaction between peoples and immigration each became more frequent, boundaries were often thought of more complexly. But people continued to think of national identities in terms of "chosen people" and "evil others." And these further changes didn't necessarily result in immigrants being welcomed. I think of the prejudice my Irish ancestors suffered on first arriving in the United States, and the Chinese Exclusion Act in the early part of the last century.

More recently, we find what can be a contradictory and confusing picture. Global communication and transportation have brought even greater exchange both of commerce and of people. And often we have seen a lessening of the past's extreme nationalistic tendencies. But this loss of boundary absoluteness has also brought new uncertainties and tensions. Today's weakening of traditional cultural dictates—including unquestioned group identities—has for many people been disorienting. And not everyone has benefited equally from these changes. The more privileged have generally prospered, while those further down the economic ladder have often suffered, sometimes badly. Today these circumstances are compounded by the highly polarized political climate that so often defines the social landscape. It is not surprising that the immigration question can today provoke such strong emotions.

How would we expect Cultural Maturity's changes to impact this evolving picture? If what I have suggested is correct, then the beginnings of Cultural Maturity–related changes are likely contributing to this more fluid reality with its easily unsettling demands. But new understandings that come with these changes should also help us better address those demands. Images like that of the semi-permeable membrane that I offered earlier point toward how we might think about borders—and with them the immigration question—more constructively. Instead of warring polar belief systems, we get a continuum of right responses that become different depending on when and where one looks.[4]

There is also the specific way in which Cultural Maturity's changes alter collective identity that I noted briefly in Chapter Two. There I observed that we should see two almost opposite-seeming kinds of change with regard to larger scale collective identity—and more specifically with boundaries. On one hand, we should see a further extension of history's outward reach. And, at the same time, we should find a new appreciation for the local and particular. These changes could begin to reconcile the immigration question's competing goods. As we become even more connected globally, we should become more deeply appreciative of the world's rich diversity of traditions and beliefs. And as we again better recognize the importance of place and the more immediate kinds of human connectedness, we should find a renewed valuing of—and sense of identity in—neighborhood, city, region, and country.

The overlapping, "nesting bowls" picture of social organization that I described also helps add detail to our task when it comes to borders. Earlier, I emphasized how it would require that we leave behind the chosen-people/evil-other assumptions of times past. In the end, it would also require the ability to craft multifaceted arrangements of context-specific semi-permeable interfaces.

All of this reveals an easily surprising but now familiar result when it comes to addressing the immigration question. While making immigration's needed more complex boundary-related decisions could easily seem beyond us, the same apparent paradox that I've emphasized with previous topics again comes into play. This new picture is more complex and demanding, but there are also ways in which what is being asked of us is really quite straightforward—indeed, common sense. Needed choices ask only that we do our best to make the yes and no decisions that best support vital lives and healthy societies. Because the kind of simplicity that results requires that we get beyond the kind of either/or thinking that before in our history has defined the working of human intelligence, it makes demands that we are not used to. But if the concept of Cultural Maturity is correct, the challenge with immigration is not unique. Bringing systemic perspective to the immigration challenge is but another part of the more general new common sense needed today in all parts of our lives.

---

4   The fact that in the end there is no clear dividing line in another way supports the recognition that polarized views are more products of how we

Integrative Meta-Perspective and Boundaries More Generally

National boundaries can easily seem a rather abstract concern for many people—or at least be a kind of concern that seems better left to formal policymakers. To appreciate the common-sense nature of how Integrative Meta-perspective alters our relationship to boundaries, it can help to recognize that the same kind of greater boundary sophistication that I've described between nations also becomes newly important with boundary relationships between every other kind of human system.

For example, I've noted how Cultural Maturity's changes make it possible to love in more complete ways. Such more Whole-Person love, as with Whole-System relationships between nations, requires that we be newly conscious of boundaries. In times past, clear cultural dictates about dating, love, marriage, and parenting made the larger portion of relational boundary decisions for us. Whole-person love also requires us to be responsible in a world where relational yeses and nos appropriately take a greater variety of forms, and often more dynamic and multifaceted forms.[5]

We see related changes with relationships of all kinds. Friendship in a culturally mature world similarly requires that we hold relational yeses and nos more dynamically and systemically. More traditionally, we might have thought of friends as people who will always have our backs, and contrasted them with enemies. In a culturally mature reality, we leave behind this two-halves-make-a-whole, mythologized kind of reality. I can count on my best friends not just to call me out if they think I'm wrong, but also to simply to be who they are in my presence. We see something similar in relationship between culturally mature or-

---

think than what is in fact the case.

5   It is a topic I address in detail in my book *On the Evolution of Intimacy*. See Charles M. Johnston, MD, *On the Evolution of Intimacy* (ICD Press, 2019).

ganizations. With human systems at all scales, we are needing to more consciously hold them as systems, and also to engage other systems as whole systems.

The way this more encompassing picture brings together the more Whole-Person/Whole-System nature of culturally mature identity, the importance of understanding boundaries more complexly, and how relationships are changing in our time helps summarize the new task with immigration. Cultural Maturity makes immigration questions about conceiving of collective identity in the most complete and life-affirming ways. Put another way, it challenges us to base our boundary decisions on the choices that are most consistent with ultimate bene-fit—on the degree to which, at particular times and places, boundaries best support societies as living systems. This section's further reflections simply add that both identity and the most life-affirming boundary decisions are always in the end also about relationship.

CHAPTER SEVEN

Sexism, Racism, and Other Forms of Bigotry—Reexamining the Foundations of Identity

We confront some of the most visible social polarization today with issues that involve inequality and bigotry. Increasingly, sentiments translate into the ready allegiances of "identity politics." Identity politics is most explicit with the populist Left in advocacy for women's rights, with LGBTQ concerns, and with efforts to address racial injustice. But where we encounter identity politics with the populist Right, it just as much defines absolutist positions. It is then more likely to be voiced by blue-collar and rural populations and defined in terms of locale, class, educational level, and economic circumstances.

Polarization that has its roots in inequality and bigotry is today some of the most important to address. It is also a kind of polarization where, at least for me, it is often not fully clear just what might best foster needed next steps. Support for equal rights, and with it the importance of confronting bigotry, has had a major place in my work. Certainly the Institute for Creative Development strongly supported progress on these fronts through policy papers and trainings. But this thread in my life began much earlier. I helped start a free health clinic for Native Americans in Seattle while in medical school, marched for civil rights in the seventies, led a think tank of African American leaders in the eighties, and consulted in South Africa at the time of Nelson Mandela's release from prison. Throughout this time I was a strong voice for gay and women's issues. And in my writings, I've emphasized repeatedly how being alert to the damage economic disparities inflict and bridging the gap between the world's economic haves and have-nots will be key to any kind of future we will want to live in.

Given this background, I have been surprised to often find myself less than wholly enthusiastic when it comes to current efforts. Any attempt to raise questions of equality, however simplistically conceived, will in a limited way have my support. At the least, in its intent it will be consistent with the long arc of history and the general direction of change that the concept of Cultural Maturity highlights. But frequently I have not been able to get as fully behind advocacy we encounter today as I would expect—and that parts of me would prefer.

With many of the topics I have addressed in this book, it has been shortcomings on the Right that have been most obvious. Arguably with identity politics this remains the case. Ideological assumptions from the Right can translate explicitly into racism and sexism. But here I will often give greatest attention to potential blindnesses on the Left. If nothing else, because they are less acknowledged, they are especially worthy of attention. But I think it is the case, too, that, at this point, awareness of such blindnesses may be particularly important if we wish to move forward in our thinking.

Let's start with current women's rights advocacy. I wrote about both important contributions and concerns in my book *On the Evolution of Intimacy*. There I observed that I see the #MeToo movement and the like continuing a critical trajectory of change and alerting us to essential recognitions. But I also noted that simplistic conclusions too often go unchallenged. I cite as an example people's tendency with accusations of sexual misconduct to lump together behaviors and circumstances that should not at all be painted with the same brush. I affirmed the unquestioned importance of calling out violating behaviors that should have been condemned years ago. But I also emphasized the need to think with greater nuance about violation and to do everything possible to get the evidence required to make needed distinctions.[1]

I've mentioned how, on the Left, populist political correctness too easily translates into tripwires for the unwary. Some of those most prevalent in academia concern gender-related questions. These same limited assumptions are today often accepted without question by those on the Left. In *On the Evolution of Intimacy,* I included a whole chapter on "Lessons for Men and Lessons for Women." I describe how, as we take on the challenge of understanding identity and love in more complete, more Whole-Person ways, important new tasks exist for everyone. I've found it fascinating how often the simple—and really quite obvious—observation that needed learnings go both ways has proven controversial. I concluded that chapter in the book with the observation that, depending on the maturity we bring to engaging today's profound new gender- and sexuality-related questions, the result could equally well be major new depths of mutual understanding between men and women or an exacerbation of the historical battle of the sexes not unlike the growing polarization we find today in other spheres.

I've often found myself with related mixed feelings with recent advocacy that focuses on racial equality. I totally support the general direction of change proposed by the Black Lives Matter movement and

---

[1] From the book: "The most obvious lumping together has happened between kinds of implied misconduct in the workplace. Publicized examples have ranged from rape and extreme abuse of power, to lewd and clearly inappropriate behavior, to instances where, if there was any transgression at all, it was minor and by all evidence unintentional. And situations that had nothing to do with workplace power discrepancies, but rather with social relationships and dating, also quickly ended up being tossed into the same pot."

similar efforts. But again, it concerns me how often efforts are framed simplistically. As an example, the current rallying cry to "defund the police" is at the least clumsy in its articulation.[2] There is also how, in a similar way to what we find in academia with questions of gender, calls for greater dialogue are too often accompanied by taboo topics where stepping over lines of political correctness can have immediate negative consequences.[3]

It is quite possible that efforts on all of these fronts will prove ultimately positive. In that they raise concerns that are consistent with changes that need to happen, even when simplistically conceived, they should help move issues along. But the fact that we so often see the unquestioned acceptance of reactive assertions makes me concerned that we may be witnessing some of the same regressive dynamics that I've observed with other topics. It is with identity politics that we see extreme populist sentiments on both the Right and the Left today taking most explicit expression.

---

2   Ultimately, it may prove an obstacle to meaningful change. Several times over the years, I've done think tank processes with law enforcement groups around the future of policing. One of the themes that has always emerged is that police are not happy having to be the front-line resource with problems that they really didn't have the tools to address—such as mental health issues, addiction, and homelessness. I've long been an advocate for funding community mental health systems that would be the more appropriate means for carrying out this kind of social function. As far as the police, this might mean some reallocation of funds. But ultimately, we need better policing, not a posture that simply makes police the enemy.

3   And some of the unacceptable topics are particularly pertinent to making progress. In the think tank I did with black leaders, I remember one conversation about police violence in which a respected participant reminded the group that many more young black men died at the hands of other black men in the streets of Chicago each year than in the whole country at the hands of police officers. The simple observation that solutions might require shared responsibility has become unacceptable in the traditionally liberal media. And an observation like this black leader made would be wholly taboo.

Distinguishing Kinds of Change

In asking myself why I might feel less than wholly supportive of many current efforts, the kinds of observations I've just made capture a major part of the answer. It bothers me to see what can feel like a growing acceptance of simple-answer ideological purities. But there is also another contributor. Because it brings this chapter's needed larger question into focus and helps further clarify what responding effectively to current circumstances ultimately requires of us, it is worth taking time with. The additional contributor also helps put current efforts in historical perspective and highlights important reasons why what is being asked of us might easily seem like too much.

In Chapter One, I observed that some changes needed in our time are best thought of as extensions of Modern Age goals, while others reflect Cultural Maturity's further developmental steps. The larger question with issues of equality and bigotry has to do with personal identity, about how as individuals we best understand what ultimately makes us who we are. The achievement of equality in the basic sense of rights and opportunities gets at a part of the answer, but it is best thought of as a culminating task of the Modern Age project. We heard its goals first clearly articulated in the U.S. with the Bill of Rights. And gradual progress toward its realization has defined much of social advancement over recent centuries.

The important recognition for this inquiry is that the identity task with Cultural Maturity is about more than just this. Cultural Maturity highlights the importance of a new, more Whole-Person/Whole System sort of identity. This recognition doesn't in any way diminish the importance of success with the Modern Age project. But it does suggest that ultimately more than just this will be needed. The additional contributor as far as why I can feel less than fully enthusiastic with identity-related advocacy in our time is the fact that the larger part of such advocacy remains focused on Modern Age objectives.

This distinction has important implications both with regard to how the objectives are described and for the task of formulating effective change strategies. There are multiple ways we could come at understanding it.

One of the simplest when it comes to advocacy on the Left concerns how such efforts tend to focus on equivalence and dismiss questions of difference. Note how in gender discussions the topic of differences between men and women is largely taboo. One of the best ways to be censured in the academic world today is to imply that real differences may exist. (It is worth noting that while academics might find assertions about gender differences unacceptable, the average kindergarten teacher will find the claim that there aren't differences rather silly.) In a similar way for the Left, the only legitimate explanation for differences in the circumstance of racial groups tends to be bigotry.

Once we venture into Cultural Maturity's more Whole-Person/Whole-System territory of experience, we find equal interest in similarities and differences. Indeed, it is observations about differences that often have the most practical implications. My observation that today's gender-related conversations could equally well result in mutual understanding or an exacerbation of the historical battle of the sexes is directly related to this distinction. Mutual understanding hinges on our being able to appreciate both our shared humanness and ways that our lives may be particular.[4]

---

4   Looking at differences in any detail is well beyond our scope, but Creative Systems Theory does more specifically address them. With regard to gender, the theory proposes that while there is immense individual variation—indeed, that it is common for men to manifest more of the feminine than the average woman, and the reverse—we find on average a 60/40 balance between more archetypally masculine and archetypally feminine qualities relative to gender. It also fills out this observation by delineating the predictably different ways that gender archetype–related

A formal Creative Systems Theory notion that I touched on in Chapter Two helps tie this observation to the distinction between Modern Age goals and the tasks of Cultural Maturity more conceptually. It also ties it more directly to the question of identity. The Myth of the Individual describes how the way that individuality has been framed with Modern Age belief stops fundamentally short of identity in the Whole-Person/Whole-System sense. In the end, it is two-halves-make-a-whole identity and based on projection. When we project, we see stereotypes. The important recognition as far as difference is that these stereotypes can just as readily involve the knee-jerk responses of bigotry or an ideology-based denial of differences. Understand identity in more complete ways and we find the kind of equal interest in similarities and differences that I have described.

The Trap of the "Angry Victim"

I find one observation particularly helpful for identifying when advocacy from either the Right or the Left falls short—at least with regard to change of a culturally mature sort. We hear it taking the form of "angry victim" narratives. The essential recognition is that even where such narratives have their roots in real oppression—as they commonly do—they all too readily get in the way of what effectively dealing with oppression will ultimately require.

---

characteristics manifest with various personality styles. With ethnicity, suggesting that any kind of difference might exist can be even more controversial. Here, the theory observes that we see variation in the personality style patterns that are most prevalent with people of various ethnic backgrounds. These differences are again not great, but I've written about how the differences that do exist have implications as far as what ways of addressing inequities might provide greatest benefit. And with reflection, the fact that differences might exist becomes rather obvious. While I'm a good musician and a decent athlete, I've never pretended to be as naturally gifted in these realms as so many of my black friends. See the Creative Systems Personality Typology in *Creative Systems Theory*.

What I am suggesting in highlighting the angry victim narrative could easily be misinterpreted. I don't in any way intend to diminish appreciation for actual harm, whether perpetrated in the past or today. I include this observation because it helps fill out understanding with regard to what is needed going forward. In addition, in highlighting a specific way in which current efforts may stop short of where we need to go, in a perhaps surprising way it supports being optimistic about future progress. The article that follows is drawn from a series that began with the piece that I included in this book's Preface.

I've proposed that the ultimately all-too-similar populist beliefs of the Right and the Left today put us at major risk. A red flag for the presence of such beliefs is worth noting. We find people assuming the posture of the angry victim. We must take some care with this recognition, as it can produce conclusions that misrepresent circumstances and that can be used in ways that perpetrate harm. But the recognition can also help us bring important nuance to our understanding.

I've written extensively about the importance of acknowledging real limits. In the face of complex realities, it is important to be as clear-eyed as we can be not just about what is possible, but also about limits to what may be possible. Acknowledging the fact of limits when they are real is central to engaging choices in ways that can work going forward. A common response when we deny limits—one that all too frequently gets in the way of efforts to effect change—highlights the importance of this kind of acknowledgement. Frequently in the face of real limits we end up identifying as victims, and more specifically, as angry victims.

The "offending" limit may be to how quickly some change can happen or simply how complex realities often in fact are. The response can seem reasonable. Real and significant victimization may have taken place. And when appropriate, anger can serve to drive change. But identifying as the angry victim is a specific kind of response with ultimately unhelpful consequences. The person ends up speaking not from the whole of themselves, but from a reactive psychological **part.**

Certainly, any degree of mature engagement then becomes impossible. But effecting any meaningful kind of change also becomes very difficult. People who identify as victims tend to project aspects of themselves onto the world and see others only as oppressors. In doing so, they give away their own authority. And often the people they demonize are exactly those they claim to want to affect. At the extreme, as any good psychologist recognizes, people who view themselves as victims are some of the most vulnerable to themselves becoming victimizers.

I've noticed something unexpected in my years doing therapy and training leaders. We would expect people to most identify as victims when oppression is most severe and the oppression is obvious. In fact, people then tend to fight and struggle to improve their circumstances as they can. Instead, the time when we are most likely to find strong identification with victim narratives is when the larger part of the oppression has resolved.

Why might we then encounter this dynamic? The answer lies with how the victim narrative serves to protect people from vulnerabilities that come with the necessary next steps in growth. Previously, identifying the offending force as outside oneself and calling it to task has been a key step toward becoming empowered and taking action. But when the needed change processes reach their later stages, often needed change depends as much on recognizing one's own responsibilities in the tasks that remain.

The fact that we commonly find victim narratives with identity politics—and in particular with its extreme populist versions—at least alerts us to how such advocacy can stop short of what is ultimately needed. Understanding how the victim narrative works also helps further clarify just what the needed larger task involves. I am less certain about whether the more specific observation about when we are most likely to encounter victim narratives applies with what we see today, but if it does, that recognition too has significant implications.

As far as how the victim narrative serves as a signal that advocacy stops short, the important recognition is that identifying either as an oppressor or as a victim, by providing beliefs that are very hard to question and a sense of connectedness with those similar to ourselves, protects us from having to take on identity's new demands. The oppression may be very real, but beyond this, perceptions become based on projection, with the identities of the victimizer and the victim each being perversely dependent on one another. More specifically with regard to how victim narratives limit us, while in a certain sense we can feel empowered by them, when we find identity in a self-righteous association with victimhood, in the end we reinforce the images of powerlessness that we claim to want to escape. When we make everything about oppression, it becomes very difficult to see beyond it.

As far as how understanding the victim narrative helps us make sense of the task going forward, we come back to how Cultural Maturity's challenge in the end is to realize identity of a more complete, more

Whole-Person/Whole-System sort. We can also be more specific as far as how the task of getting beyond the victim narrative applies both to the Right and to the Left. With identity politics of the Right, the perceived oppressor is educated coastal elites. With identity politics of the Left, it is right-wing bigots. In either case, moving forward most obviously requires those who oppress others getting beyond finding identity through feelings of superiority. But it is also the case that the most powerful levers for change often lie with those who might perceive themselves as victims refusing to take part in the assumed polar relationship. This completeness of identity has not before been an option, but its possibility follows from Cultural Maturity's cognitive reordering and will eventually be essential to effectively moving forward.

For the question of whether what I've noted about when we are most likely to encounter victim narratives is pertinent, we find at least limited evidence. Common indicators of when change processes reach this point have become increasingly acceptable parts of the social conversation—such as people emphasizing micro-aggressions, holding onto images of trauma (and often trauma from times well past), and seeming to compete with others for who should be thought of as most oppressed. While none of these indicators are definitive, we witness all of them today with identity politics on both the Right and the Left. A friend and colleague offered a useful metaphor for the kind of trap the angry victim narrative represents. She described it as like picking at a scab. There is the illusion that it accomplishes something when in fact it only makes healing's completion more difficult.

Again, we need to be careful that observations such as these about psychological dynamics, whether about victim narratives more generally or about current circumstances, don't get used in ways that only have us repeat old blindnesses. But because the victim narrative can so directly be an obstacle, it is important that we be alert to where it may be coming into play. And if the further possible dynamic that I've noted plays a significant role, in suggesting that we may be further along in our efforts than we might have imagined, it could point toward a kind of hope.

Black poet Toni Morrison offers a good way to think about what the needed greater completeness of identity requires from the side of those who have been oppressed. In noting James Baldwin's observation that black writers tend to write as if they have a white man on their shoulder that they need to convince, she described how she tries to write "without the white gaze."[5] I think the fact that she succeeds in doing so is a major part of what makes her writing so effective. While the white inner critic has origins in real oppression, as often today, put in Parts Work terms, it exists as an unhelpful part. One essential implication is that while oppression as it exists in the present without question needs to be addressed, past a certain point changes on the part of the perceived oppressor can only in limited ways rid one of the feeling of being oppressed. That requires re-owning projections and learning to live "without the white gaze."

Addressing issues of equality and oppression requires everyone involved to engage identity more systemically. That includes people who have oppressed getting beyond the need to project less-savory parts of their makeup onto others who are different from themselves. It also includes those who have been oppressed being sure they are not projecting their own authority (and with this the place within themselves from which they judge worth and identity)—that they are not giving away the power to affirm that indeed they matter.[6]

---

5   This was a repeated theme in her work. It can be found articulated by Morrison with particular clarity in the film "Toni Morrison: The Pieces I Am" by Timothy Greenfield-Sanders.

6   Creative Systems Theory offers that we might be more specific. Bigotry involves an identification with "upper pole" sensibilities and projecting and denigrating "lower pole" dynamics. (This is particularly common in people who themselves have felt denigrated in other contexts and experience their "upper pole" identities as threatened.) Victim narratives involve identification with "lower pole" sensibilities and projecting and

Bringing Pieces Together

This chapter's various reflections come together with more general observations that I have made with each of the book's previous more topic-specific chapters. Certainly we again see direct challenges to both the Right and the Left. The challenge to the Right when it comes to bigotry is most obvious. Bigotry with regard to gender, race, sexual orientation, or people with disabilities has simply stopped being an option. While the direct challenge to the Left can be less obvious, it is particularly key to healing current divisions. We similarly need to get beyond dismissal and denigration on the basis of class, educational level, and kind of employment. People on the Right have a point when they accuse educated elites of hypocrisy when it comes to issues of discrimination.

More specifically with regard to the challenge of culturally mature perspective, again we see how needed steps forward, rather than just making past assumptions problems, challenge us to expand how we think. As an example, when it comes to solutions, the Left traditionally has tended to emphasize the need to rectify oppression, while the Right has put greater emphasis on accountability. Along with confronting the limits of past beliefs, bringing culturally mature perspective to addressing inequality and bigotry also requires recognizing that each of these historical contributions is also part of the solution.

We can use the importance of appreciating both similarities and differences to add detail to this more systemic picture. The Right historically has tended to focus on difference, but it has been difference of the absolute sort, and difference that makes one group better than another. The Left has tended to focus on sameness and found any sug-

---

denigrating "upper pole" dynamics. Getting beyond either kind of pattern requires the owning of both polar aspects— "upper pole" and "lower pole"—as parts of one's own complexity.

gestion of real differences unacceptable (while at the same time denying that its own position can be denigrating toward others). Using the language of Parts Work, the needed no to the Right is the simple recognition that bigotry no longer serves anyone. The yes to the Right is the recognition that appreciating difference still has a place, only now it is real difference—the difference of seeing accurately—not the manufactured and mythologized difference of bigotry. The no to the Left is the recognition that making everyone the same—whether with some unisex ideal or a lumping together of humanity's rich diversity—in the end only gets in the way of knowing either ourselves or anyone else in ways that ultimately serve us (and that dismissing the views of those who don't agree with its particular version of sameness is its own kind of bigotry and only compounds the problem). The yes is the recognition that we are in fact all in this together. In the end, we discover that the complementarities created by our multihued differences make life full and complete in ways that otherwise would be impossible.[7]

Once again, we also see how moving forward effectively requires all the new skills and capacities that inherently accompany culturally mature leadership. Certainly a new, more ultimate kind of responsibility is key. Whole-Person/Whole-System identity makes each person newly responsible for engaging life from the whole of who they are. We become responsible for appreciating both ourselves and whoever we may encounter not as symbols, but simply as people. We also again encounter the importance of better acknowledging both complexity and uncertainty. The whole-box-of-crayons nature of Whole-Person/Whole-System identity means that advancement requires a more conscious

---

[7]   Note how this reframing ties to the Creative Systems Theory observation that polarity at its most basic contrasts difference on one hand with unity on the other. Here the Right has traditionally identified with absolute difference, the Left with absolute unity. Culturally mature perspective challenges us to appreciate how difference and unity are themselves aspects of a more complete picture.

acceptance of reality's many-hued multiplicity. And the inherent dynamism of the new picture makes the fact that things have never been as clear-cut as we might have assumed inescapable. The fact of real limits also again necessarily comes newly into play—at the least with how the absolutist beliefs of times past necessarily limit us. With victim narratives, we also encounter a more relationship-related kind of limit. We find limits to what the oppressor and the oppressed (in their often codependent relationship) can be for one another.

The ability to better appreciate the role of context also has an important place in needed new capabilities, here in particular the role of time in determining what is true. For example, denial of the fact that realities evolve often plays a major role in supporting the victim narrative. We find illustration today on the Left with how gender discrimination can get framed in terms of an eternally oppressive "patriarchy"[8] and with suggestions that nothing has really changed in race relations—with extreme assertions, since the time of slavery. On the Right in the U.S., we can find animosities that have changed little from the time of the Civil War. While unquestionably a great deal remains to be done on all fronts when it comes to addressing inequalities and bigotries, dismissing what has already been achieved is a clear indicator of simplistic thinking. It is also the case that when we cynically deny progress that has been made, our thinking in fact undermines the possibility of mak-

---

8   In *On the Evolution of Intimacy,* I describe how the term "patriarchy" makes useful sense only if understood in the context of culture's evolution. Understood in this way, the term also has very different implications when it comes to advocacy. Creative Systems Theory emphasizes the importance of getting beyond the archetypally masculine dominance of Modern Age realities and learning to think in more integrative ways. But it also makes clear that regarding patriarchy as some "evil other" is evidence of ideological—and ultimately unhelpful—thinking.

ing further real progress. When our focus is on the past, it is very hard to move forward.[9]

An important question brings us back to an essential systemic observation that has run through this book. I've noted that it is less that the issues we face today are creating polarization than that ideological polarization is creating the issues, or at least how issues appear—how it is division itself that ultimately most divides us today. With identity politics, we tend to focus on the fact of sexism, racism, or issues of class and assume it is the cause of both pain and societal tensions. And, certainly, to a major degree, it is the culprit. But it is worth asking just how much of the division we experience currently may also be a product of the more general division splitting societies. If such larger systemic mechanisms—in combination with the regressive dynamics that I've noted—in fact play a major role, the implications are significant, at least with regard to strategy.

---

[9]   Understanding bigotry and oppression in the context of time requires two kinds of recognitions that are often missed. First, we need to appreciate that bigotry and oppression have been with us since humanity's beginnings. Slavery was extremely common in early societies (including in Africa well before the European slave trade), and it has been rare that people have not in some way denigrated others that they perceive as different from themselves—whether the difference is a product of class, ethnicity, gender, educational level, sexual orientation, or individual limitation. We also need to appreciate where attitudes have evolved. With concerns of the Left, since the turn of the last century in the U.S., we have seen groundbreaking civil rights legislation; for women, the passage of the Nineteenth Amendment and major strides toward equal opportunity in the workplace; the legalization of gay marriage and the inclusion of people of diverse sexual orientations in the military; and a growing recognition that accommodations for the disabled are an essential part of healthy societies. With concerns of the Right, in a similar way, we need to appreciate how often in fact the American Dream historically has worked, bringing true prosperity to the less educated and advantaged. And in recent years, we've finally begun to take seriously disparities that are a function of locale, kind of employment, and class. While much more needs to

If the primary problem is the literal fact of oppression, then the most powerful strategies will focus directly on alleviating it. But if today's more general division is creating a significant portion of what we witness, then we need at the least to revisit assumptions. Directly addressing bigotry will still have a critical place. But it could well be that much real change can come with strategies that focus on broader change processes.

A Step Forward

I'll end with a story that comes from work with a client who had been bullied as a child. Its concern is more particular than the broad cultural dynamics this chapter has focused on. And I don't intend it as a prescription for where we should currently be at. It could too easily be interpreted as a suggestion that when it comes to trauma we should just "get over it," something that would only return us to old denials. But the story does shed light on where a rethinking of oppression and bigotry has the potential to take us. And in keeping with what we have seen with other topics, it points toward a picture of the possible that is ultimately both practical and empowering. It further illustrates how Integrative Meta-perspective frees us to be most effective in the choices we make. It also further fills out the role of context in culturally mature understanding, in this case context in the sense of here-and-now, personality style differences.

My client had been severely abused by a bully in his growing up. Now in his forties, he continued to see the world as unfair and abusive to him. One result was that he often felt depressed and commonly undermined himself while rarely recognizing the role he was playing in what he felt. He also had a hard time being around people who at all reminded him of the bully.

---

be accomplished all the way around, denying real progress in the end only reinforces old narratives.

In one session when he felt particularly stuck he again brought up the bully. I asked my client a couple of questions. First, I asked if he would rather be the bully, have the bully's personality style. (Certain personality style relationships almost inevitably result in bullying.) He realized in thinking about it that the most important pleasures in his life came from things that his own particular personality style was good at and attracted to. He said "no," that he would rather be himself. I then asked him if he would prefer that all the people in the world with the bully's personality style would disappear. After time to reflect, he saw that he would not want that either. In fact, people with that personality style tend to do things with their lives that my client really didn't enjoy doing and was not very good at. He saw that he would be poorer for their absence. Those two simple questions took my client a long way toward fully owning his authority and making the contribution he was capable of.

It is not my intent in suggesting a relationship between simple bullying and more historical kinds of abuse like sexism and racism to in any way dismiss the depth and significance of more historical kinds of oppression. They are not the same. But the example does illustrate an essential kind of change that can alter one's experience dramatically. I am reminded of a favorite quote from Nelson Mandela: "There is no passion to be found playing small—for settling for a life that is less than the one you are capable of living." Note that my client's insights did not at all deny the very real oppression and the pain it had created. But they did illustrate how it is possible to get to a place where the past does not continue to inflict pain in the present and get in the way of moving forward effectively.

CHAPTER EIGHT

Science and Faith—The Rewards of Systemic Understanding

Over the course of history, it is the juxtaposition of the material with the spiritual that people have most often associated with polarity. In modern times it takes expression in debates between science and religion, as we saw manifest with particular celebrity a century ago in the Scopes Trial's pitting of evolution against divine creation (and Clarence Darrow against William Jennings Bryan). Today, the Right in the U.S. relies on the nearly unquestioning support of Evangelical Christians while those on the Left, though often religious, are much more likely to have confidence in science.

I include the science versus faith polarity in this book's reflections in part because for many people it is this polarity that feels most basic. I also include it because of how it can seem impervious to larger ways of understanding. If it is indeed possible to engage the science/faith polarity in a way that is more encompassing, that is no small thing. In addition, I include science and spirituality for a couple of reasons that help fill out this book's particular perspective. The way in which this polarity gets close to polarity at its most fundamental helps us more deeply grasp what polarity itself is ultimately about. And the way a creative frame invites us to entertain larger ways of thinking about both science and religion provides important support for Creative Systems Theory's particular approach.

We appropriately start with the hard, larger question. A person might assume it to be, "Is God real?" It is this question that has conventionally divided thinking into two mutually exclusive, irreconcilable realities. But as I will come back to shortly, in fact I don't find it terribly helpful. This is not because I know the question's answer, but rather because it is limited in where it can get us (unless we are willing to settle for endless circular debates).

The better question concerns the nature of truth. Over the course of history, the contrasting perspectives of science and religion have provided our bottom-line answers when it comes to truth. Sometimes the forms these answers have taken have spoken in concert; at other times they have manifested as warring opposites. But in the end, the juxtaposed vantages of science and religion are what we have come back to. Our larger question becomes, "Just what is it that ultimately makes something true?"

For most people, the whole idea that it might be possible to get beyond the science versus faith debate and engage the truth question in larger ways makes little sense. Or if the possibility is entertained, the assumption is that the answer would be so philosophically obscure and complex as to be of little practical value. But there is another legitimate explanation for why we might have a hard time imagining other possibilities. It has to do with how we have been capable of thinking in times past—with how understanding has worked and been structured.

A common experience when people do Parts Work supports this explanation. People of more scientific inclination will tend to assume, at least initially, that a part that thinks rationally and scientifically appropriately sits in the Whole-Person/Whole-System chair. But it is not too long before the person realizes that this conclusion doesn't really hold up. While the rational part contributes powerfully, there are many concerns, and concerns of no small importance—such as purpose, love, or wisdom—for which it has little of great value to say. The person also sees that recognizing how this part is limited in what it can offer, however initially disorienting, will be key to growing in any deep and meaningful way.

Something very similar tends to happen for people who identify with more spiritual inclinations. This may be an individual with quite traditional religious beliefs, a person with more humanistic "spiritual but not religious" tendencies, or someone of more New Age bent. Commonly the person will assume that spiritual truth appropriately sits in the Whole-Person/Whole-System chair. Again, for them, this is not an unreasonable conclusion. For the person of more traditional religious beliefs, this is where historically we have found connection with kinds of knowing that we have assumed to be omniscient and omnipotent. If the person is not so expressly religious, this is where we experience the essence of things, the "core" of truth.

It can take longer for the larger realization to sink in with people of more spiritual/religious inclination, but if they work long enough, in a similar way they recognize that the assumption that spiritual truth appropriately sits in the Whole-Person/Whole-System chair also stops short. The person comes to see that while the spiritual part has much of great importance to contribute, it alone is not enough. In a well-lived life—a spiritual life in the best sense—the more manifest parts of existence are as important as the essences. Indeed, it turns out that spiritual parts can fully come alive only to the degree that the more manifest aspects are given equal attention. The person also realizes that this recognition, however initially disorienting, will be key to growing in any deep and meaningful way.[1]

---

[1]   If the conclusion that the more manifest parts of existence are as important as the essences is not obvious as stated, some brief reflection on the association of essence with some "core" of experience helps make it more concrete. The important recognition is that aspects of experience that manifest closer to the surface layers of experience—more on the pe-

In doing Parts Work, the chairs that advocate for more material and spiritual sensibilities each have much to add to the Whole-Person/Whole-System chair's reflections, but they are at best consultants. When we miss this essential fact, ultimately unhelpful—indeed, dangerous—specifically ideological conclusions result. With Parts Work, people confront this fact not just as some abstract conclusion, but personally and immediately. People find that if either a more material or the more spiritual part sneaks into the Whole-Person/Whole-System chair, not only do they end up with unhelpful and divisive big-picture conclusions, they become vulnerable to making misguided day-to-day choices.

Applying a Creative Frame

Creative Systems Theory lets us go further and address how the material and the spiritual might relate more conceptually. It is not essential that the reader agree with this particular interpretation. For our purposes with this book, it is enough that the theory further supports the fact that more encompassing perspective might be possible. But for those who have interest, there are important added reasons to take time with how the theory approaches the science versus faith question. It not only helps fill out the book's more general focus on polarity and its implications, it brings clarity to one of the most essential recognitions if we are to understand the workings of polarity deeply.

I've described how polarity at its most fundamental, rather than contrasting two kinds of difference, juxtaposes unity and oneness on

---

riphery—are ultimately just as important to the experience of meaning. This conclusion is affirmed in a particularly striking way with the recognition that people with different personality styles variously hold excitement closer to the core or closer to the periphery of the body. Thus, to equate truth with some "core" of experience is to create a "chosen people" ideology. See the Creative Systems Personality Typology in *Creative Systems Theory*.

one hand with difference and multiplicity on the other. We can apply this conclusion directly to the polarity of science versus religion. Science in its various forms over time can be thought of as having its origins in how the world looks from the difference/multiplicity side of fundamental polarity when experienced at a collective scale. Spirituality/religion in its various forms over time in a complementary way has its origins in how the world looks from the unity/oneness side of fundamental polarity when experienced at a collective scale.[2]

In my book *Quick and Dirty Answers to the Biggest of Questions,*[3] I addressed the science versus religion debate and reflected on how CST's creative frame offers a way to begin to get beyond it. The following is adapted from it with a few additions made where further detail is pertinent to this book's inquiry:

Our next ultimate question is the most frequently debated. Here we turn to the often-conflicting views of science and religion. Most crudely our question asks, Which interpretation is right? The better question might be, How do the material and spiritual relate to one another—if they do at all?

---

[2]   To avoid confusion given the particular emphasis on political polarization in this book's reflections, I should address why if science has to do with difference, the political Right today is so dismissive of it. Addressing the topic in depth requires more of Creative Systems Theory than it makes sense to include here, but there is a simple way to put it. While science and religion have given expression to ultimate polarity through the larger part of culture's story, in our time, the difference/material aspect of ultimate polarity is in fact more defined by business and economics. Scientific truth set in opposition to economic truth today becomes a polarity in which science makes the more left-hand contribution. We can see this with how science is pursued in the more reflective environment of academia while business is a more in-the-world kind of endeavor.

[3]   ICD Press, 2013.

With Modern Age thought, drawing back on Descartes, we've tended to place the material and the spiritual in separate worlds. This is not an entirely unhelpful solution. It has shielded us from conflicts so fundamental that giving them voice has resulted in people being burned at the stake. But this is not a solution that can satisfy for long. Descriptions that depend on two mutually exclusive explanations can't, in the end, be sufficient. Any ultimately compelling picture must be of a more overarching sort.

The more systemic vantage provided by Cultural Maturity's cognitive reordering at least supports the conclusion that encompassing perspective should be possible. And Creative Systems Theory's application of a creative frame provides a specific way to get there. Creative Systems Theory proposes that not only do the material and spiritual aspects of experience relate as aspects of something larger, the way they relate reflects what most fundamentally makes us human. It also proposes that in spite of how often the relationship between science and religion through history has appeared adversarial, all along the two have been engaged in an evolving conspiracy.

Observations about the basic architecture of polarity help clarify the underlying relationship. The theory describes how polarities juxtapose more right-hand, archetypally masculine characteristics with qualities of a more left-hand, archetypally feminine sort. In science and religion we find ultimate expressions of these polar proclivities as they manifest in culture as a system. Science is about collective right-hand sensibility in its purest expression. Religion is about collective left-hand sensibility, similarly cleansed of contamination by the right. Put another way, science gives expression to the "difference" half of ultimate polarity at a cultural system level, religion to ultimate polarity's complementary "connectedness" dimension.

A closer look at the contrasting contributions of science and religion supports this interpretation. Science is about distinction—this as opposed to that. Biology delineates the creaturely into taxonomies of genus and species, chemistry gives us the periodic table and the interplay of atoms and molecules, and classical physics describes objects of differing mass and the action-and-reaction laws of material cause and effect. Spiritual/religious experience in contrast highlights oneness. We can think of religious belief through history in terms of four connectedness-related themes: how existence arose from the undivided ("in the beginning"), community (congregation and communion), right thought and behavior (shared moral assumptions), and how experiences interrelate (and, in the end, how it all interrelates). In Latin, *re-ligare*, the root of the word "religion," means "to connect." William James put it this way: "In mystic states we both become one with the Absolute and we become aware of our oneness."

We can use the language of narrative to help bring this creatively framed systemic picture more to life—both to make it more palpable and to animate it, to put it in motion. Cultural Maturity's cognitive changes help us step back not just from who we are as creative, toolmaking beings, but also from our natures as tellers of stories about how creation works. We can think of science and religion as history's two great "creation story" storytelling traditions.

All cultures have their stories of how things originally came into being. And most include, too, ways of accounting for events that followed, the amazing and mysterious emergence of life, as well as the immense new creative capacities that arrived with conscious awareness. We can think of all of history's great encompassing stories as versions of this story—told in ways appropriate to their time, place, and perspective.

Our past stories have taken the forms they have in part because of each time's practical circumstances (for example, the invention of the telescope resulted in a dramatic challenge to past belief). But even more they have taken the forms that they have because of the developmentally specific sensibilities that at different times have ordered our worldviews. Our early animistic and much later Enlightenment interpretations were different not just because of *what* we knew, but because of *how* we knew. In present times, that translates into the Big Bang and Darwinian evolution on one hand, and on the other, into modern monotheistic religion's various accounts of a spiritual genesis.

A creative interpretation of the science/religion polarity helps us appreciate how these two narrative traditions have also taken the forms they have because of the internal vantages from which they have been told. Religious/spiritual traditions have observed creation's story from a more left-hand creative vantage, and from the more nonrational (and connectedness-loving) aspects of intelligence. Science has simultaneously observed creation's story from a complementary more right-hand vantage, and with the more concrete and rational (difference-biased) aspects of intelligence. An integrative evolutionary picture alerts us to how, all along, science and religion have been observing a single story.

We can use this creative interpretation to add important detail to our thinking. For example, it helps us make sense of how the realities of science and religion have evolved. I've described how culture's larger creative narrative has progressed from a time of archetypally feminine dominance in our tribal beginnings toward our Modern Age in which archetypally masculine proclivities come to hold sway. As we would predict from this description, we see a parallel progression over time from realities defined almost wholly in spiritual terms with our animistic beginnings, toward what we find today, a world in which many people hold strong religious beliefs, but in which more material values (scientific, but even more that this, economic) have ultimately the greater influence.

We can also use a creative frame to map the changing relationship of science and religion over time. In early societies, material and spiritual sensibilities tended to be spoken of almost as one. Later, as with much of the European Middle Ages, material and spiritual inclinations more often took expression in ways that were explicitly at odds. Later still, as with Cartesian dualism, science and religion more comfortably coexist, but they accomplish this feat by, in effect, ignoring each other's existence. This sequence of juxtapositions is just what we would expect to find if the relationship between science and religion is ultimately creative.

In Chapter Ten, we will examine how the unity/oneness and difference/multiplicity halves of fundamental polarity juxtapose in evolving ways not just over history, but also over the course of any human developmental process. Truth, at least as we can know it, becomes an evolving expression of this ultimately creative relationship.[4]

---

[4]   Thinking of science and religion in terms of juxtaposed pure polar tendencies in fact represents a simplified picture. More accurately, at any specific time and place, scientific and spiritual beliefs reflect creative balances of archetypally masculine and archetypally feminine tendencies perceived in polar terms. For example, while we might think of science as a pure expression of the archetypally masculine, with early science we always also find a fair bit of the archetypally feminine. Aristotle saw divine action as what began it

The God Question and Today's Related Challenge to Science

I've promised to return to my perhaps surprising assertion that the "Is God real" question is really not that useful. A person might assume that my reason for this conclusion is the one commonly put forward by self-described atheists, namely that efforts to rationally prove the existence of God through history have never quite succeeded. But while I would generally agree with this observation,[5] my reason for setting aside the "Is God real" question could just as well be thought of as coming down on the opposite side of the argument. It has more to do with the poverty of atheism as a concept. While the religion versus atheism debate certainly sells books, I find atheism as a belief a bit silly. The vehemence we commonly find with its adherents suggests that it is best thought of as but another form of fundamentalism. More specifically, in leaving out the evolutionary dimension of understanding, the argument for atheism doesn't really hold up.

If I argued, indeed became obsessed with arguing, that the ancient Greeks were wrong for believing there were gods atop Olympus, or that tribal societies have been wrong for having animistic deities, you

---

all—the "unmoved mover"—and invisible causal forces behind consequences of every sort. And medieval alchemy was mysticism as much as it was objective inquiry. With religion we find the opposite. While spiritual sensibilities in our tribal beginnings were almost purely of a left-hand sort, over time, religion has become increasingly institutional and codified, as much a function of material structures as it is of things magical and ephemeral. It has also become increasingly a sphere of experience in which individual interpretation has a legitimate place.

5 Documenting this conclusion is well beyond our scope. But I think it accurate that rational arguments through history—whether those of Plato and Aristotle, Thomas Aquinas, or René Descartes—have proven, if not ultimately circular, are at least insufficient.

would appropriately conclude that I had missed the point. While these are kinds of beliefs that tend not to work today, in their time they gave expression to an important kind of need—and more deeply, I would argue, reflected an essential aspect of human sensibility. I agree, as the advocate for atheism may be quick to point out, that the more modern idea of a monotheistic God with a capital "G" has resulted in harm as well as benefit. But as I see things, the larger portion of that harm, while it may have been done in the name of religion, has come not from religion *per se*, but from our systemic need for worlds of us and them. And while it is true, too, that religion makes little sense rationally and can lead to some claims that really don't hold up, that is not what is important. Religion through time has given expression to essential aspects of being human, aspects that are just as important in our time, and arguably now more important than ever. Religion as we have known it in Modern Age times is best thought of not in terms of the rightness or wrongness of its assertions, but as one chapter in an evolving picture of truth.

In challenging atheism's critiques of religion in this way, it is important to note that Creative Systems Theory just as directly challenges science. And here again the challenge is not what we might imagine. At least it is different from that commonly put forward by the Right—that science is just another kind of belief or opinion. Science represents a very specific kind of belief with radical and powerful implication. Its foundation—repeatable, objective observation (proof by experimentation)—at least for certain kinds of understanding takes us beyond simple opinion and gives us a solid foundation from which to make choices. The observation commonly made today that it is fine to have your own opinions but that you don't get to choose your own facts holds up well when it comes to questions where science applies, and represents one of modern science's profound contributions. The challenge to modern science is the simple recognition that not all concerns are fully amenable to its method. And that includes a great many of our times' most important concerns: the nature of human purpose, the deep workings of intelligence,[6] creativity, and relationships of all sorts being just a few of the numerous examples.

From Integrative Meta-perspective's more systemic vantage, science and religion, material and spiritual become crayons in the systemic box. Using the Parts Work analogy, the yes to science is an affirming of the precision and detail it brings to certain kinds of understanding. The no comes in response to the recognition that while it can provide clear answers for particular kinds of questions, with others, it can blind us to what is ultimately important. The yes to religion is that appreciating connectedness is often critically important and has particular importance in our time. The no comes with the recognition that connectedness is at best half of what makes truth true, and that failing to appreciate this fact leaves us just as blind to what is ultimately needed.[7]

---

[6] The scientific method is extremely limited when it comes to addressing anything beyond what is understandable with intelligence's specifically rational aspects. Concerns that are better addressed using emotional intelligence (with its particular pertinence to human relationship), the more imaginal parts of intelligence (that give us dreams and myth), or the intelligence of the body (that informs our sensory and sensual lives) will, for the most part, lie beyond its reach. The significance of this observation comes into particularly high relief with the recognition—central to the thinking of Creative Systems Theory—that our multiple intelligences, working together, are key to what makes us human. Chapter Ten will more directly address this more complete picture of intelligence and its implications. In the end, understanding any Creative Systems Theory concept deeply requires drawing on the whole of intelligence's multiplicity.

[7] Parts Work's second cardinal rule—that parts don't talk to parts—provides further valuable insight when it comes to the contributions of science and religion. In addition to recognizing that neither the science chair nor the religion chair gets to sit at the center of things, the person also learns to recognize how "crosstalk" between the science and religion chairs similarly leaves us short. This kind of internal debate had a function in times past. Indeed, as I describe in *Creative Systems Theory*, we can understand each of history's previous views of how the material and the spiritual relate in terms of it. Such direct conversation between parts gave

Where Culturally Mature Truth Takes Us—and a Look to the Future

I've observed that if it is indeed possible to engage the science/spirituality polarity in a way that is more encompassing, that is no small thing. These reflections point toward how it may be that the historical battle between science and faith can indeed be reconciled. They also suggest that doing so need not require endless pages of philosophical argument. Integrative Meta-perspective makes separate-worlds views unnecessary. And a developmental picture makes clear that however irreconcilable the conclusions of science and religion have often seemed, ultimately they have been in collusion. Creative Systems Theory proposes that all along they have been working together to drive the creative evolution of human values and human understanding.

In wrapping up, we should return to what I have proposed is the needed larger question when addressing science versus faith polarity: What is it that ultimately makes something true? Given Creative Systems Theory's observation that the conclusions of both science and religion are ultimately partial, it is only fair to ask just how the theory answers the truth question. Creative Systems Theory agrees with the claim often made with postmodern interpretation that what we can know for sure—in the sense of just what is "out there"—is limited at best. But it doesn't stop with this acknowledgement. It suggests that there is a lot we can say about how we know, about the cognitive lenses

---

us the easy complementarities of more magical thought (as with yin and yang in classical Chinese belief), the warring absolutes of medieval dogmatisms, and the separated-worlds assumptions of Cartesian dualism. But Creative Systems Theory argues that it has no value going forward. The result with Integrative Meta-perspective is a more encompassing and dynamic understanding of identity and truth. Specifically for science and religion, we get a picture in which each becomes part of a larger reality, and through which we make sense of our worlds. It also points out that the ways of knowing we have available to us change over time. With these additions, truth becomes whatever defines the growing edge of understanding, the perceptions that at a particular point in time are most generative, that most work to make us "more." Put more conceptually, the theory makes truth whatever is most ultimately creative. In our time, truth becomes such creative rightness held with a degree of awareness and completeness not before an option.

In keeping with what we might expect for truth understood from the vantage of Integrative Meta-perspective, this more creative definition brings together all of the new skills and capacities that I have referenced in previous chapters. Certainly, drawing on truth in this sense involves a new completeness of responsibility. It explicitly demands not just responsibility for making choices correctly, but also for the truths on which we base those choices. And inescapably, a creative picture of truth confronts us with complexity (the importance of considering all the crayons in the systemic box) and uncertainty (how, in a creative reality, it is never possible to fully know just what will come next). A creative picture of truth also repeatedly brings us face to face with the fact of real limits. Creative decision-making is never about freedom in the sense of limitlessness. Rather it is about the more mature and powerful kind of freedom that comes with learning to make choices while acknowledging the fact of real limits. Creative truth is also quite specifically about appreciating the role of context. It is about truth not in some abstracted, eternal sense, but truth at specific times and places. Today, it is an expression of understandings whose time has now come.

Again, we encounter our familiar apparent paradox. While this more encompassing answer to the question of truth asks more of us, if

at the same time becomes newly filled out and able to contribute in more complete and vital ways.

we can tolerate it, there are also ways in which it is more straightforward than what we have known. In our time, truth becomes what results when we draw consciously on the whole of who we are. Arguably the truth task then in fact becomes simpler, though an essential recognition that I've pointed toward repeatedly is needed for this observation to fully make sense. Ideology makes truth simpler because in perceiving only with parts of ourselves we are protected from being overwhelmed by life's complexities. When we draw on the entirety of understanding's systemic workings, we get a picture that is more straightforward—and ultimately simpler—because it better reflects all that is involved. Add a creative frame and we better understand how all of this might be so.

What should we expect for science and religion in the future? If Creative Systems Theory is correct and the relationship between science and religion is indeed creative, certainly we should expect to encounter increasing fascination with more integrative formulations. Exactly what such formulations will look like is beyond what we can determine from our present vantage—no matter how far along our thinking may be. We can know that culturally mature perspective doesn't let either science or religion off easily. Beyond that, if this basic interpretation holds, we can be certain that new formulations should be increasingly systemic, in ways that affirm the ultimate richness of being alive, and more specifically of being human.[8]

---

8   We can perhaps go a bit further. In *Creative Systems Theory,* I fill out the theory's approach to understanding science and faith and take a shot at applying the theory to predicting the future of each of them. As we would expect when we leave behind polarized understanding, the picture that results, along with challenging science and religion fundamentally, also helps us more deeply appreciate the contributions of each.

CHAPTER NINE

Rethinking Human Advancement

The book's last topic-specific chapter brings each of those previous together. Its defining question is "How in our time do we best think about human advancement?" Again we find a topic that easily splits people along ideological lines. But it is also a topic that so clearly needs to be answered systemically that simply pursuing it in a committed way helps get us past historical divides.

We'll start by looking at what a definition of advancement sufficient to our time might look like. We will then briefly examine what keeps the needed new definition from seeming obvious when old definitions so clearly no longer serve us—including a look at a contributor that today is significantly amplifying the dangers. And finally, we'll turn to solutions, both needed personal recognitions and more institutional approaches that might support the kind of change necessary if our choices are to in fact result in real steps forward.

Advancement and Our Modern Crisis of Purpose

In Chapter Three, I spoke of culturally mature truth as having process and content aspects and promised to give more attention to the content dimension. The previous chapter made a start in describing how a creative frame helps us get at such truth at its most basic. Here our interest lies with what makes something true in the sense of what we draw on collectively in making decisions—the measures we use to make social choices. The topic of advancement includes the kinds of questions that we've more commonly addressed with concepts like wealth and progress.

While most obviously a big-picture concern, how we conceive of advancement also has more immediate and personal implications. I introduced my book, *Hope and the Future,* with a description from therapy I had done with a young man who had attempted to hang himself. It became strikingly clear in our conversations together that the hopelessness he felt was only in limited ways personal. More it was about the state of the world. He described having a hard time thinking of a future he would want to be a part of. I gave that book the subtitle, "Confronting Today's Crisis of Purpose."[1] The aspects of therapy that most helped my client involved examining together what a meaningful human future might look like, exploring how we would need to rethink the human story to get there, and him asking how in his life he might contribute to that new story. I could just as appropriately have given *Hope and the Future* the subtitle "Confronting the Need to Rethink Advancement."

What does reconceiving wealth and progress look like? In modern times, we've defined wealth as the accumulation of material assets. And we've most often defined progress in terms of new inventions and economic growth. These definitions are so familiar that we rarely question them. But, today, if we don't question them—and question them fundamentally—the consequences could be dire. The central recognition if our definitions are to work going forward is that they must be of a more whole-box-of-crayons, systemic sort. While this statement might seem to suggest that we need newly complex formulations, it is equally true that we find—as we have found with the more specific topics of previous chapters—that needed new measures are really quite common sense.

When I want to help someone address the advancement question, I will often first engage the person at a personal level. I will ask them to talk to me about what creates meaning—"wealth" in the largest sense—in their individual lives. Most people mention money, but most recognize that beyond a certain point money stops being significant in the same sense. Invention, too, most always has a place—people like their gadgets. But most people appreciate that other things are ultimately as important—or often much more important: one's family, one's friends, one's community, one's felt relationship with nature, one's health, one's creative and intellectual pursuits.

People doing this exercise are often surprised to find that a significant mismatch exists between what they have described as most important for a meaningful life and many of their day-to-day choices. I may joke with the person as they confront this mismatch, pointing out—only partly tongue in cheek—that such discrepancy would seem to be almost the definition of insanity. When working in therapy, this kind of recognition can result in people making major life changes.

If the person has interest in the larger, cultural-level question, I may then engage them in the same kind of inquiry with regard to how collectively we define wealth and progress. People tend to come up with lists that are very similar, both in being more encompassing and in better reflecting more basic needs. The fact that current world priorities reflect a related kind of mismatch becomes hard to escape. Too often today we apply an outmoded definition of advancement that excludes much that is in fact most important to us. And just as we appropriately think of individuals who make choices that are not in keeping with

---

1   In briefly introducing the idea of a Crisis of Purpose in Chapter One, I noted how we find marked increases today in rates of depression, addic-

what they find most significant as deranged, the implications are huge. In Chapter Ten, I will describe how taking our Modern Age definition beyond its timeliness threatens to leave us irreparably distanced from much that most ultimately matters to us.

More whole-box-of-crayons measures will be needed not just if we are to conceive of advancement as a whole usefully, but also if we are to effectively engage almost any more specific critical task ahead for the species. Certainly, they will be required if we are to successfully assess the benefits and risks of new technologies. (We need more encompassing measures if we are to effectively determine what we are to call benefit.) They will similarly be critical to making good environmental decisions. (It is only through them that we can appreciate how impoverished further environmental destruction would leave us.) And more mature and systemic measures for wealth and progress will clearly be necessary if we are to effectively address the ever-widening gap between the world's haves and have-nots. (Ask about benefit more consciously and we begin to better recognize not just how such disparities are ethically troubling, but how they risk destabilizing societies and putting everyone's well-being in peril.)

It is important to appreciate how fundamentally different a more systemic definition of wealth and progress is from more traditional measures. This is the case in two main ways. In contrast to Modern Age definitions, it is more consciously arrived at. The old measures came part-and-parcel with Modern Age assumptions. And there is how more systemic conceptions of advancement are more complete, both in terms of taking into account more factors and in more deeply drawing on the whole of who we are.

More specifically as far as the focus of this book, such measures are different from those implied by more ideological views. We've seen how more ideological conclusions—including those of the Right and

---

tion, and suicide.

the Left—draw on particular crayons in cognition's whole-box-of-crayons complexity. Thus they cannot by themselves provide adequate guidance. We confront even more clearly consequential differences when it comes to the views of the Right and Left if we extend them to the kind of populist extremes that we so often encounter today. Such thinking is not just ideological, it is utopian.

Utopian conclusions, in blinding us to the fact of limits, present particular dangers. We encounter other kinds of utopian views today that in their own ways can be just as troublesome. Techno-utopian solutions for the future at least blind us to the fact that what we can do is often not what we should do. And while more spiritually utopian beliefs, from images of a second coming for the chosen to New Age notions of collective realization, may not so directly put us at risk, they at least leave us blind to the complexities of what our times ask of us.

In contrast, culturally maturity measures of advancement, in drawing on the whole of our human complexity, step beyond simple-answer ideological advocacies of all sorts. And of particular importance, they leave behind the easy seductions of utopian solutions. We come back to how Cultural Maturity's more "grown up" picture is ultimately common sense. The measures that culturally mature perspective draws on simply ask us to be more fully attentive to all that matters to us.

We can draw on some of the tools that I've applied with the previous more topic-specific chapters to bring more detail to how we understand needed new measures for advancement. For example, we can identity pertinent yeses and nos with regard to traditional beliefs of the Right and the Left. The yeses for the Right include support for values such as individual rights, the well-being of families, private property, national boundaries, and free markets. The nos include traps that come with moral rigidity, with anti-government sentiments, with extreme materialism, and with conclusions that too easily result in inequality and bigotry. The yeses for the Left include concern for social justice, respect for the environment, a valuing of multiculturalism, and attention to how government can be used to address societal ills. The nos for the Left include the dangers of excessive government bureaucracy, identity politics contributing to cultural divisions, the perpetuating of beliefs that undermine authority and see boundaries as problems, and a post-modern relativism that can get in the way of making essential distinctions.

We also encounter each of our now familiar new skills and capacities when we begin to apply more systemic measures for advancement. Once again, we confront the double responsibility that comes with Cultural Maturity, in this case not just for succeeding at advancing, but for fundamentally revisiting what it means to advance. And in making needed discriminations, we face the importance of being more comfortable with the complexities of a multifaceted world, of accepting that uncertainty necessarily intrudes into our considerations, and of acknowledging the fact that real limits exist to what might be possible. And being attentive to context again derives new importance, in particular being attentive to how what makes something advancement is relative in cultural time. Here we've seen how our times require fundamental new steps in our understanding of just what advancement entails.

So What Is the Problem? And a Major New One

Given that new ways of thinking about advancement are so obviously important—and ultimately not complicated—it is reasonable to ask why it can be so difficult for people to get their minds around even the simple fact that anything new is needed. We've faced the main reason repeatedly in these pages. The needed new definitions challenge traditional assumptions. And in requiring us to think in new ways, their implications can easily overwhelm us. Regressive dynamics—and the extreme polarization that today so often accompanies them—can also get in the way of needed recognitions. It can be hard to understand how anything beyond warring idealized—and often utopian—visions are needed, much less make needed headway with the required more encompassing and creative conversations.

It is worth taking time with a more specific contributor to the difficulty that today may play a particularly consequential role. In the Preface, I included "misuse of emerging technologies" in my list of significant dangers as we look to the future. We find a good example in how our ever-more-clever electronic devices can be two-edged swords. Several ways in which this can be the case have critical pertinence to these reflections. They are important to recognize because in each case we find effects that get in the way of seeing clearly what our times ask of us. Understanding in each case also sheds important light on where needed solutions lie going forward, irrespective of what kind of ideological traps we may be most vulnerable to.

In working with young people today, I find it rare not to encounter addiction to electronic devices—with boys most often to video games, with girls more to social media. I think of device addiction as both a symptom of today's Crisis of Purpose and a significant driver. Some professionals hesitate to use the word "addiction" in this context, but I think that it is important to do so, so that we accurately understand the problem. The rapid-fire stimulation of video games and the "likes and clicks" of social media, by offering electronic substitutes for real fulfillment, directly mimic the mechanisms of addiction. Addictive substances work by providing the feedback and affirmation normally provided by feelings like excitement, power, or pleasure while requiring none of the vulnerability needed for the real thing. For years it was a dirty secret of high-tech companies that they were optimizing programs for these addictive effects. But such effects really don't require malevolence—addiction is a much more reliable way to get attention than providing content that actually benefits us.

A further concerning effect has gotten particular attention of late. It relates more specifically to social media. At the very least, social media algorithms by their nature create distortion and "fake news." It has been well documented that the soap opera of sensationalized content (and outright lies) is much more likely to attract eyeballs—and more likely to trigger search algorithms—than real news. But there is also a further dynamic that relates more specifically to the digital collection of information. As far as amplifying polarity, it may prove even more significant. And in a similar way, it does not require malevolence and easily sneaks up on us.

Every time we make an online choice, the record of our choice then influences the kind of information that we receive. This result might seem benign—even helpful. We only get the kind of information that we have interest in. But it also means that increasingly we get different information that pushes us into silos of belief. And the tendency is toward increasingly extreme and ideological belief. Using our box-of-crayons metaphor, crayons become ever-more amplified and distorted in their hues. We don't need Russian or Chinese hackers to set us against one another. We are doing it with the cleverness of our digital toys.

Very intelligent people are setting off alarm bells about this effect. Some technology experts are proposing that it might be the primary driver of modern polarization and absurdity. I think of it more as exacerbating deeper processes that had already been well underway, but I nonetheless find it of real significance. Part of the reason this further dynamic warrants concern is the fact that social media has become such a central part of many people's lives. But there is a greater reason: No obvious way exists to counter the effect. Simple laws can't get us there. And the only ultimately effective option if social media companies wanted to accept the needed responsibility would be for them to give up their advertising-driven business model, something that they are very unlikely to do. The best the technology gurus have to offer as a solution is to suggest vaguely that something has to happen at a cultural level. The widely viewed Netflix film "The Social Dilemma,"[2] which lays out the argument for such dangers ends with this conclusion.

The need to confront this conundrum brings us back to the larger solution this book is about, and also to the topic of this chapter. The observation that solutions need to happen "at a cultural level" might seem only to shirk responsibility. But in the sense that technical fixes don't ultimately provide necessary solutions, it is accurate. For these reflections, the important recognition is that the concept of Cultural Maturity provides a way to understand what needs to happen at a cultural level. We need the kind of perspective—and wisdom—that comes with culturally mature understanding. More specifically as far as this chapter's focus, we must come to think about advancement in ways that give us the insight and courage to say yes to what is ultimately important and no to dynamics that don't really serve us.

This more specific kind of solution has both more personal-level and more societal-level aspects. At least the personal level solution should now be clear. What I observed with my client who had attempted to hang himself highlights what is needed. I noted that the parts of therapy that most helped my client involved examining together how, in our time, he might live a purposeful life. When I work with someone who suffers from addiction—whether to substances like heroin or alcohol, or with device addiction—in a similar way effective therapy depends on helping the person find real significance that can replace the pseudo-significance the drug or activity has provided. People are then better able to grasp how the drug or activity is robbing them of the things that in fact most matter.

More societally, the kind of psychological changes that I've described with Cultural Maturity's cognitive reordering should bring a

---

2   A 2020 American docudrama directed by Jeff Orlowski and written by Orlowski, Davis Coombe, and Vickie Curtis.

growing awareness of the importance of making more systemic choices. As far as influences of any kind that today can get in the way of appreciating what is needed, they should also make us better able to recognize when we are being exploited and make such exploitation increasingly unpalatable. The antidote lies with a simple recognition: The best way to confront harmful influences is to create enough contrast that such influences come to be experienced for what they are, at the least as distraction, but even more, forces that do direct damage to what is ultimately most important.

With this kind of perspective, the fact that we can't get rid of damaging effects that might result with electronic media by legislation or policy, while still of major significance, becomes less of a dead end. In working with clients, I often point out that the most precious thing we have is our attention. Societally, whether our interest is personal well-being or the health of social systems and the species, we have to choose to not let our attention be hijacked and manipulated.

More Institutional-Level Implications

If we are to effectively make such discriminations, we need social structures able to address advancement-related questions with the needed sophistication. One of the most striking characteristics of contemporary society is the degree to which we have lost trusted agents. I've noted how decades back we had people like Walter Cronkite and Edward R. Murrow, who we could count on to at least communicate the facts. Today we find a crisis of confidence in leadership of all sorts. There may be no more important question as far as our future well-being as a species than what it might mean to again have trusted agents. At a cultural level that means somehow we must establish social structures and ways of thinking that can function as culturally mature trusted agents.

This chapter's extended reflection is intended less as a proposal than simply to stimulate the imagining of possibilities. In *Creative Systems Theory*, I ponder the future of institutions of all sorts—educational, economic, religious, scientific, governmental. In looking at government, I offer a possible decision-making approach as a thought experiment to help people think more creatively about future governmental structures. It is pertinent to rethinking societal structures more generally. And as a bonus, it invites us to think about alternative ways to address the needs voiced today by populist advocacy. I quote from the book:

All of this leaves us with a pivotal question: Will a needed next stage in the evolution of governance require radically new governmental forms? It is hard to know. Conceivably all of the needed changes that the concept of Cultural Maturity suggests could happen through the modification of forms we already know. But effective government going forward will certainly require a deep rethinking of how our forms work, and engaging more systemic ways of understanding them. It will also require getting beyond current government-related absurdities such as the partisan shrillness that can make arriving at effective policy nearly impossible and the extreme hold that money has on governmental functioning.

Lately, I've found myself reflecting on one very different kind of structure that in various forms could have a critical role with a next chapter in the story of governance. Something like it may become not just essential, but almost inevitable if we are to successfully make our way. The image's inspiration comes from think tank groups I've led through the years.

This new kind of structure would be a deliberative body that is given the task of engaging essential future questions from a post-partisan, culturally mature perspective. This new kind of structure could function as, in effect, a fourth branch of government (in the U.S.—whatever would be the equivalent in other countries), though to work, it would not need to have formal authority.

The idea has inherent complexities that might seem to immediately derail it—most immediately, concerns about just how membership in the group would be determined and how the group would relate to the other aspects of government. But if its authority came wholly from the power of its contribution— the degree that it effectively functioned as that trusted agent— such concerns disappear. Note too that making its role advisory also means that there is no reason we should be restricted to only one such group (or limit such groups to particular spheres). In addition, it means that we don't need to wait for such deliberative bodies to be established by legislation. Everything we need exists right now. And with today's Crisis of Purpose, their significance could be recognized more quickly than we might imagine.

I offer this description only as conjecture, but it points toward an important kind of rethinking. Particularly in more informal manifestations, such mechanisms could have application not just with governmental decision-making, but also with education, religion, science, and more. It is not inconceivable that Cultural Maturity's changes could make related efforts—in different forms at different times and places—a commonly accepted part of leadership.

Thinking about how such deliberative bodies might function brings attention to a kind of "bridging" that has important implications for the broader topic of leadership—that between more top-down and more bottom-up leadership approaches. For this book's reflections, it has particular pertinence to the more specific leadership challenge of finding constructive ways to address what the best of populist sentiments bring to the table. It might seem that what is most important in establishing such bodies is finding the people who can provide the needed culturally mature leadership. And often that would be the case. But because their effectiveness would depend on the broader acknowledgement of their contributions, in the end they could work only to the degree to which there is sufficient "culturally mature followership." At the least this means people able to appreciate and support the conclusions of such efforts. But in most cases it would also mean people throughout society being willing to provide input and in different ways be active participants. It would be important that structures be designed with these kinds of possibilities in mind.

Notice an important kind of implication. Such bodies could in potential serve to draw on the larger intelligence of society in ways that were promised by the Modern Age democratic experiment, but which the mythologized assumptions of times past have often kept us from fully realizing. They also suggest the possibility of addressing the needs highlighted by modern populism, but now not in a manner that collapses into ideological sureties and utopian simple-answer thinking, but in more Whole-Person/Whole-System ways that draw on society in its entirety.[3]

---

3   It has been suggested by serious thinkers that groups tasked with major aspects of decision-making could be selected randomly from society. That is not what I am suggesting, though there are circumstances where it might be appropriate. Random selection risks only having top-down decision-making replaced by an equally limited bottom-up alternative. Selection of participants in most decision-making processes would require careful consideration consistent with the specific decision-making task. At the very least, we confront the fact that culturally mature decision-making is unlikely unless groups reflect sufficient Capacitance. (Creative

This is just one kind of idea—and again, only a thought experiment. My point is simply that we need to envision structures that can once again serve as trusted agents—only now trusted agents able to provide guidance in a culturally mature world. Doing so necessarily starts with recognizing that the polarized and polarizing ideological solutions of times past inherently leave us short. It comes into focus with this chapter's more specific task, learning to think of advancement more systemically, in ways that better take into account all that matters to us. And it takes concrete form in working creatively together to arrive at structures and processes that can support this larger good.

Today's regressive polarization amplifies the need for new kinds of trusted agents at all levels. I've noted how, with respect to government, Cultural Maturity's changes may be needed not just so that we can rethink government, but so that we don't end up destroying the structures we have now. Certainly the transitional processes that the concept of Cultural Maturity argues will be needed to effectively move forward will require trustable ways to stay allied with more systemic measures of advancement.

Systems Theory describes how culturally mature understanding is Capacitance-dependent.) And in some cases, quite specific and exceptional expertise would be necessary. That said, there are circumstances where selection processes that draw randomly from a population could produce useful results, particularly if the group had access to outside resources and consultation. Especially with more local issues, it could have a place. One strength with random selection is that it provides a simple way to have decision-making processes reflect a population's diversity.

CHAPTER TEN

Further Conceptual Reflections—
The Roots of Polarization and the
Cognitive "Growing Up" on Which Our
Future Depends

I've promised to provide more detailed conceptual observations for those who might find them of interest. They are not needed for the book's basic argument to hold and to make sense, but readers who would like more solid theoretical underpinnings for the book's approach may appreciate the added insights. Many of these observations draw more specifically on the thinking of Creative Systems Theory.[1]

First, we will look in greater depth at possible causes for today's extreme social and political polarization, with particular emphasis on factors pertinent to the concept of Cultural Maturity. Next we will turn to questions that relate more specifically to the role of polarity in how we think. We will then more closely examine the cognitive reordering that produces culturally mature understanding. And I will conclude with a small handful of Cultural Maturity–related summary topics—including brief reflections on the evidence we have for the concept's accuracy, on just what Cultural Maturity's changes accomplish, on the concept's per-

---

1   Each of the Creative Systems Theory–related observations can be found developed in more detail in *Creative Systems Theory*.

tinence to the question of hope, and on Cultural Maturity's long-term implications.

How Did We Get Here?

In Chapter One I described multiple possible explanations for the extreme social and political polarization we witness today and promised to return for a closer look at potential contributors—in particular possible factors that are especially relevant to this book's reflections. I've emphasized how the implications could be very different depending on the reasons for what we see.

To begin, I observed that what we witness could be a product simply of the two-steps-forward-one-step-back way change has always worked and noted that this may very well be adequate explanation. Periodic times of social polarization pretty much come with the territory of having collective lives. If this is the primary cause, then a simple effort to be more level-headed should pretty much take care of things.

But I also described how the explanation could be more concerning. What we see today could be a product of regression in the face of today's new challenges. I've noted how human systems commonly regress when they feel overwhelmed. If this regression is limited, then being patient and finding needed perspective could be a sufficient solution—at least if we can avoid reacting in ways that have us make destructive choices.

But what we see could also be a product of regression of a deeper and more consequential sort. If we are seeing major regression, then times ahead could be particularly demanding—and at times particularly crazy. Indeed, it is possible that we could fail at what is being asked of us with catastrophic consequences. There may be very little we can do.

Of particular pertinence for our inquiry in these pages—and also for legitimate optimism as we look to the future—I also noted possible stressors that in different ways are themselves products of Cultural Maturity's changes. With the book's topic-specific chapters now behind us, many of these further contributors should now make fuller sense. Certainly we would expect today's loss of familiar guideposts as culture's past parental dictates abandon us to be disorienting. There is also how Cultural Maturity's cognitive changes confront us with questions that before now we could not have tolerated. We've seen how addressing them will demand new kinds of skills and capacities. We've also seen how these new questions often require that we think and relate in ways that before now would not have made sense to us. Any of these demands could further contribute to the experience of overwhelm and the ideological tensions we experience today. And together they could contribute considerably.

But as I've emphasized, many of the stressors that risk overwhelming us are products of the same changes that ultimately offer a way forward, and this has important implications. If they do play a role, there is reason to hope. And our task becomes clearer: doing everything we can to bring not just courage, but needed, more mature ways of understanding to bear.

I've also pointed toward a further possible Cultural Maturity–related contributor in noting the particularly absurd nature of so many of today's ideological assertions. As making full sense of this possible additional contribution requires some big-picture perspective that we do not yet have, I will wait until after the next section's look at polarity and the workings of formative process to address it conceptually. But a simple analogy helps make the connection. I've observed how we find developmental parallels between the challenges presented by our time in culture's evolutionary story and those that come with the second half of life in an individual lifetime. Midlife tends similarly to be a time of confusion—and often a bit of craziness.[2] If these parallels hold, there

---

2   Studies show that forty-seven is the age when people are most likely to describe feeling desperation and a lack of direction in their lives.

could be further reasons inherent in how change processes work that could make beginning to engage Cultural Maturity's changes feel disorienting and even desperate. But if these additional factors play roles, they can also be thought of as further supporting the legitimacy of hope. Indeed, as I will also come back to shortly, they could suggest that success in moving forward might come not just more readily than we would otherwise imagine, but also more rapidly.

Later, after we have a bit more theory under our belts, I will also come back to an observation noted earlier that provides a kind of evidence that Cultural Maturity–related factors could be contributing to what we see today that is particularly pertinent to the focus of this book. The specific kind of ideological polarization we witness—between populist camps on both the Right and the Left—is in fact predicted by how Creative Systems Theory describes the cognitive underpinnings of today's changes.

Again, I am not confident that I know which of the possible factors I have listed (or others I may not have considered) most contribute to today's extreme polarization. If I were asked to guess, I would say some combination is involved. What I know for sure is that ideological absolutism and extreme partisanship today put us at real risk. I am also comfortable asserting that something at least similar to what the concept of Cultural Maturity describes will be needed eventually—and will provide an antidote to contemporary dangers and absurdities whatever their particular origins.

Polarity and Creative Self-Organization

In introducing people to how Creative Systems Theory explains the role of polarity in how we think, I often make a provocative claim. I observe that we can get most of the way toward understanding the concept of Cultural Maturity—and ultimately Creative Systems Theory as a whole—by answering three polarity-related questions: Why do we humans think in the language of polarity in the first place? Why have we now begun to see understanding that "bridges" familiar polar assumptions? And how do we best think about what happens when we begin to leave behind ideology and think more systemically? A closer look at the workings of polarity and how they might relate to the challenges we now face provides perspective for understanding both what we see today and what will be needed going forward.

Creative Systems Theory's answer to the first question is closely tied to the theory's basic premise. The theory proposes that what most defines us as humans is the audacity of our toolmaking, meaning-making—we could say, simply, "creative"—capacities. It describes how the reason that we think in polar terms in the first place is that polarity is essential to the workings of formative process.

Creative/formative processes begin in a womb world—in original unity. The newly created thing then buds off from that initial wholeness, creating polarity in the process. Over time, the newly created entity, and polarity with it, evolves and matures, with polarity manifesting in predictable forms with each creative stage. The diagram in Figure 10-1 depicts how polarity progresses over the first half of any formative process, what the theory calls creation's Differentiation Phase.

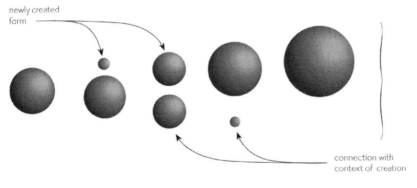

newly created
form

connection with
context of creation

CREATIVE DIFFERENTIATION

Fig. 10-1. Polarity's Evolution Over the First Half of Formative Process

The theory's answer to why now we might see the "bridging" of past polar assumptions comes with the recognition that the creative stages that bring new creation into being aren't the end of things. Once new possibility has become established, the newly created entity reengages with the context from which it was born. With creative process's Integration Phase, the newly created aspect becomes part of a now expanded whole. Over time, we come to experience the result as "second nature"—to use language I've drawn on here, as a "new common sense." The diagram in Figure 10-2 depicts formative process's two halves most simply.

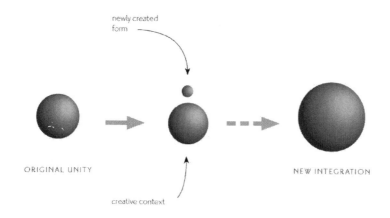

POLARITY AND BRIDGING
IN FORMATIVE PROCESS

Fig. 10-2. Differentiation and New Integration in Creative/Formative Process

Creative Systems Theory observes that we witness the same basic progression of polar relationships over the course of any human formative process, from simple creative acts to culture's evolution. Formative dynamics begin in oneness, become manifest through polarity, and then reconcile into a larger, more inclusive entirety.

For example, with a simple creative discovery, at first there is only what we have known before. Then comes excitement with a fresh insight's newness. Next that insight becomes more distinct and over time grows and develops. Then, later, we begin to experience it differently. We relate to it now as simply one part of a now expanded understanding.

We see a related sequence of creatively related polar dynamics with individual psychological development. The tasks that define the first half of a person's life similarly involve distinction, here with the establishing of identity. With childhood we begin discovering who we are, with adolescence we make our first forays into the social world, and during adulthood we establish our unique place in that world. Second-half-of-life maturation involves more specifically integrative tasks. It is about learning how to live in the world with the greatest perspective, integrity, and proportion.

Of particular importance for this book's reflections, Creative Systems Theory observes that we find this same progression of creatively related polar dynamics manifesting as predictably at a cultural scale as we do with a particular creative act or with individual human development. This observation strongly supports both the power of a creative frame and the concept of Cultural Maturity's essential conclusions.[3]

What Creative Systems Theory calls the Creative Function summarizes this basic relationship between polarity and creative/formative process. The Creative Function expands the image in Figure 10-2 like the bellows of an accordion. It describes how we can map any kind of developmental dynamic in terms of a predictable sequence of creatively ordered polar juxtapositions. The Creative Function presents a simpli-

---

3   See *The Creative Imperative* or *Creative Systems Theory* for a more detailed look at this progression.

fied picture. Stages can vary in length and emphasis depending on the kind of system and surrounding circumstances, and formative processes can be aborted at any stage. But the general sequence holds with remarkable consistency. The Creative Function provides a concise, information-filled way to depict how polar relationships evolve over the course of any human formative process.[4]

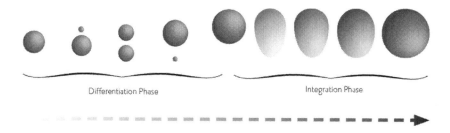

Fig. 10-3. The Creative Function

For the answer to the third question—and specifically how it pertains to our time—we can turn to any of this book's topic-specific chapters and observations about how the kind of thinking that topic requires changes with Cultural Maturity's cognitive reordering. Each topic has supported the thesis that today we confront new kinds of questions. It has also alerted us to how new ways of thinking and acting will be needed if we are to effectively address them. These new ways of thinking and acting follow naturally from Integrative Meta-perspective and the more whole-box-of-crayons view of the world that results.

---

[4]   In *Creative Systems Theory*, I describe how all the primary concepts of Creative Systems Theory are at least indirectly represented in the diagram.

Transition, the Dilemma of Trajectory, and Transitional Absurdity

I've observed that there may be something particular about our time that creates much that is most nonsensical in today's polarized beliefs, and I made analogy with midlife in individual development. To make sense of this observation conceptually, we need to turn our attention to the midpoint in the Creative Function's progression, a period that Creative Systems Theory calls simply Transition.

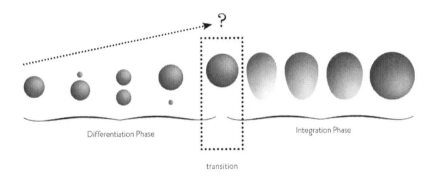

Fig. 10-4. Transition and the Dilemma of Trajectory

Transition marks the line separating the creative journey's two halves. Just because it confronts us with new worlds of experience, we would expect it to be a challenging time. But there is also a more particular reason why we might expect to behave in crazy ways at that time. Note in the diagram how, with Transition, the lower pole of the organizing polar relationship essentially disappears. To put this circumstance in perspective, we need two further Creative Systems Theory concepts, the Dilemma of Trajectory and what the theory calls Transitional Absurdity.

We can frame the Dilemma of Trajectory in terms of polarity's underlying "procreative" symmetry. The upper and lower poles in the diagram reflect more archetypally masculine and archetypally feminine aspects of fundamental polarity. I've observed how we see a progression over the first half of culture's story from more archetypally feminine dominance to realities in which the archetypally masculine has the much greater influence. We encounter something similar with the first half of any creative/formative process. The important recognition is that this trajectory of change would seem ultimately to leave us with nowhere to go.

At Transition we stand in a world of all right hand and no left, of all content and no context, of life as ultimate abstraction held ever more distant from experience's roots. Taken far enough, proceeding further in this direction threatens to sever us from much that is most important in being human. This includes the body, the child's world of imagination, our human connectedness with one another, and our felt relationship with the spiritual and with nature.

The concept of Transitional Absurdity in Creative Systems Theory describes what happens when this particular circumstance combines with all the more general challenges that come with Cultural Maturity's new demands. We then find realities that are in potential not just ludicrous, but destructive. It is beyond our scope to examine the concept of Transitional Absurdity in great detail, but it provides explanation for much of what can seem most nonsensical, and even crazy in our time.

Some Transitional Absurdities reflect "overshooting the mark"—applying outmoded, onward-and-upward ways of thinking to questions that now demand much more of us. Others keep us from recognizing that new questions even exist. Denial in the face of critical environmental challenges such as climate change provides the most obvious example. Other Transitional Absurdities more actively function to protect us from being overwhelmed by Cultural Maturity's considerable demands. The important recognition for this book's reflections is that we can think of today's extreme polarization in this way. By locking us into predictable responses, polarization provides a reliable protective mechanism. If Cultural Maturity's challenge is too much to tolerate, instead we can settle for the protective pseudo-significance of warring polar ideologies.

I've suggested that Cultural Maturity–related dynamics, along with being consistent with hope, are also consistent with the possibility that change could happen more quickly than we might imagine. We can turn again to the midlife analogy. I've noted that while a person's altered behavior at midlife can be striking in its bizarreness, the absurdity is ultimately a product of how midlife change processes work. There is also another important recognition suggested by therapy with people at this point in their lives. I've observed consistently that if the person can find the courage to take on the now timely, new developmental challenges, the absurdities tend to be relatively short-lived. If the analogy holds, changes could take place more rapidly than might otherwise be predicted.

I've also promised to come back to the observation that the mechanisms that produce Cultural Maturity's changes could be playing a role in the particular way that polarization today is manifesting—as warring ideologies of a specifically populist sort. There are multiple ways that Transitional dynamics could produce this result. The loss of culture's past parental status that happens with Transition could certainly contribute. Without a mythologized, overarching sense of authority, anti-authoritarian inclinations predictably gain influence. There is also how the Dilemma of Trajectory should make the split between haves and have-nots particularly extreme—and possibly intolerable for those who are less advantaged. This by itself could incite populist sentiments. Finally, there is how the general direction of change that produces the Dilemma of Trajectory could amplify any of these effects. As the upper pole in the diagram ceases to work as final truth, it is reasonable that we might find identification with opposite sensibilities. The fact that Transition leaves us with so little real connection with such sensibilities could make that identification particularly extreme, and often crazy. The main reasons that we confront populist extremes today could well be more immediate. But it is interesting to reflect on how there may also be more big-picture influences.

Whatever the causes of what we witness today, again we encounter a now familiar basic recognition. Cultural Maturity's changes provide a way forward. And if the Dilemma of Trajectory and Transitional Absurdities play a significant role, the effect is particularly explicit. Besides reconciling the Dilemma of Trajectory, Cultural Maturity's cognitive reordering also provides the needed antidote to Transitional Absurdities. Cultural Maturity's cognitive changes don't diminish the challenges our times present or eliminate overwhelm—indeed, they specifically add to our time's demands. But they do provide the perspective needed to deal with current circumstances and what may lie ahead in the most healthy and creative ways.

Putting Cultural Maturity's Cognitive Changes in Historical Perspective

I've used the phrase Integrative Meta-perspective to describe Cultural Maturity's cognitive reordering and promised to later examine the notion more closely. With each of the book's topic-specific chapters, we've seen some of Integrative Meta-perspective's consequences. But we benefit from some further, more conceptual understanding. Historical perspective helps provide the needed detail.

Integrative Meta-perspective is new—and fundamentally so—but each major new chapter in culture's evolving story has similarly been marked by leaps in how we understand. The leap that brought us Modern Age thought provides the most pertinent comparison. The new sensibilities introduced with the fresh artistic visions of Michelangelo and Leonardo da Vinci in the fifteenth century and later filled out with seventeenth-century conceptual formulations such as Newton's clockworks universe and Descartes's emphasis on rationality as truth's last word did more than just alter our conclusions. They reflected a whole new kind of understanding—indeed, a new type of conceptual organization.

We can summarize what then became different with the simple observation that these changes made possible a new, more from-a-balcony kind of perspective—what we commonly refer to when we use the word "objective." Everything we tend to identify with Modern Age advancement—the rise of individualism, more democratic governmental forms, the Industrial Revolution, scientific preeminence, modern higher education, and a more personal conception of the divine—can be understood to follow from this new kind of cognitive organization and the vantage it provided.

In a similar way, we can make sense of everything about culturally mature understanding—what it asks of us and why, and also why we might expect the specific changes it describes—in terms of changes in the mechanisms through which we make sense of ourselves and the world around us. Integrative Meta-perspective is related, but also new in basic ways. To fully grasp what is new, we need to give attention to both the more stepping back part of Integrative Meta-perspective and the more specifically integrative processes that give us the new depth of engagement needed for mature—wise—decision-making.

What we step back from has multiple aspects. Most immediately, we step back from ourselves as cultural beings. As we do, we become newly able to recognize culture's previous mythologized, parental status and to begin to move beyond it. But cultural assumptions are not all we step back from. We also step back from internal aspects of ourselves in ways that have not previously been possible. That includes becoming newly conscious of parts of ourselves that before we've projected—whether idealized parts as with love and nationalism, or those we have attributed to people who are different from ourselves as with bigotry and war. In the end, we step back from how the dividing of experience into opposites has permeated thinking since our beginnings.

Though it takes us a bit beyond our focus with this book, a further aspect of what we step back from has particular significance if we are to fully grasp where Cultural Maturity's changes take us and how this is different from the realities of times past. We become newly able to step back from intelligence's multiplicity. Besides the rational (in which we take appropriate pride), intelligence also has other aspects. Creative Systems Theory emphasizes the essential roles of aspects of intelligence that are more emotional, more imaginal, and more reflective of bodily knowing. It describes how each kind of intelligence works according to different mechanisms and makes different kinds of contributions.

Modern Age belief made one part of intelligence—the rational—the ideal and understanding's end point (with the romantic thread in understanding providing rationality's lesser partner in the subjective). But rationality by itself is not enough. And obviously it can't be enough if we look at all that goes into human experience and all that ultimately matters to us. Integrative Meta-perspective affirms the importance of rationality, but it also clarifies how rationality represents only one aspect of intelligence. The stepping back part of Cultural Maturity's cognitive reordering continues the direction that gave us Modern Age thought—and also in an important sense completes it. Awareness comes to stand separate from the whole of our intelligence's systemic complexity—now including the rational.

But we can't stop here. This more complete stepping back accomplishes a lot. At the very least, it calls into question the past mythologizing of collective belief. It is what makes possible postmodern perspective. But while stepping back in this way can at first feel exhilarating, it can also feel precarious. At some level we know that by itself this is not sufficient. Ultimately we are left feeling strangely distanced from ourselves. We confront the Transitional circumstances noted earlier.

To move forward, we need the further, more integrative kind of change dynamic I've just described with the two-part workings of creative/formative process. Along with more fully stepping back from the multiple aspects of our human complexity, Cultural Maturity's cognitive changes also involve more directly owning and engaging that complexity. Not only is this more integrative kind of process different from what we have known before, it finds no parallel at all in previous cultural change points. We plumb experience with a fundamentally new kind of depth. In the process, we come to more consciously and fully embody all that makes us who we are. It is this that produces Cultural Maturity's specifically systemic outcome.

As far as this book's focus, we need at least a bit of this more integrative kind of process if we are to make a solid start at getting beyond the polarized assumptions of times past. And of particular importance for the task of rethinking how we think, we need this second part of Cultural Maturity's cognitive reordering if we are to deeply engage intelligence's multiple aspects. With Integrative Meta-perspective, we are better able to recognize the world's rich complexity because we come to more consciously, and more fully, draw on this larger complexity in ourselves.[5]

Our box-of-crayons image helps bring the two parts of Cultural Maturity's cognitive reordering together. With Integrative Meta-perspective, we become newly able to step back from the diverse aspects of human understanding—in particular, polarity's interplaying

---

[5]   In a Chapter Eight footnote I observed that understanding any Creative Systems Theory concept deeply requires drawing on all of intelligence's multiple aspects. Most obviously this is true for the theory's developmental notions. The theory describes how specific intelligences are most dominant at particular cultural stages—from body intelligence in our tribal beginnings to rational intelligence with Modern Age beliefs. This is similarly the case with more here-and-now systemic concepts such as with the Creative Systems Personality Typology. Even the basic notion of Cultural Maturity makes deep sense only if we can engage the whole of intelligence's multiplicity. Creative Systems Theory argues that understanding most anything of great importance about us requires drawing on intelligence's multiplicity.

manifestations and intelligence's multiplicity—all the hues that make up human sensibility. And at the same time we become able both to more deeply access this complexity of hues and to draw on its various aspects in the most creative ways. We more consciously acknowledge and more directly draw on the whole of ourselves as systems—all the crayons in the box. With time, Cultural Maturity's cognitive reordering makes whole-box-of-crayons perspective seem like common sense.[6]

Wrapping Things Up

To bring this chapter's more conceptual reflections to a close, I will touch briefly on a small handful of further Cultural Maturity–related questions: What evidence do we have that the concept of Cultural Maturity is correct? How do we best think about what Cultural Maturity's changes accomplish? If the concept is correct, is hope warranted as we look to the future? And what are the concept's long-term implications?

Evidence is critical. If we are to draw on a concept like Cultural Maturity, we need to have confidence in the correctness of its conclusions. And evidence has particular importance in the case of Cultural

---

[6]   If we add the recognition that both intelligence and polarity organize creatively, we get the foundations of Creative Systems Theory's particular conceptual approach. Creative Systems Theory includes a notion it calls the Fundamental Organizing Concept. With culture's Modern Age and the assumption that truth was what we could understand rationally and objectively, Descartes's notion that existence is a "great machine" provides the Fundamental Organizing Concept. With Cultural Maturity's changes, we better recognize that truth, rather than being something separate from us that we can hold at a safe arm's length, is always a product of how, at particular points in time, we are capable of understanding. Creative Systems Theory describes how understanding in human systems organizes creatively. It also invites us to entertain the idea that truth as we can understand it—certainly truth in human systems—is similarly "creative." Chapter Three's look at the exploratory nature of good decision-making in a culturally mature reality and Chapter Eight's examination of

Maturity because most people will not find the notion immediately obvious. No one kind of evidence by itself is wholly conclusive, but taken together, the various kinds of evidence make up an argument that I find hard to refute.

Observations I've made with this book offer a basic kind of evidence. Some of the new possibilities I have described—such as bringing a new maturity to our relationship to death, or rethinking how science and religion might relate—are themselves products of Cultural Maturity's changes. And while many new challenges—such as the need to limit spiraling health care costs or the importance of rethinking war and peace—have more immediate origins, the fact that related new skills and capacities are needed to address them at least provides support for the importance of where Cultural Maturity's changes take us.

We find further evidence in the developmental parallels that I've noted. Argument by analogy is legitimately suspect, particularly when the argument is this far-reaching. But most people will agree that the parallels are at least intriguing, and most find the simple reference to a needed "growing up" in our time consistent with their experience. The fact that we can understand Cultural Maturity in terms of cognitive changes predicted by these parallels makes the developmental argument more concrete and robust. Here we've seen how the Dilemma of Trajectory provides particularly solid evidence for the importance of Cultural Maturity's changes. In observing that neither going forward as we have nor going back can ultimately work, it makes Cultural Maturity—or at least something that could provide a similarly integrative result—the only real option.

Some of the more immediate results of Cultural Maturity's changes can also be thought of as evidence. I think in particular of how Cultural

---

the ultimately co-generative relationship of the truths of science and religion in different ways pointed toward this more dynamic picture.

Maturity offers an answer to today's Crisis of Purpose. I've described how contemporary realities frequently leave people feeling at best confused, at worst dispirited and cynical. I've proposed that the concept of Cultural Maturity, in offering a new guiding story, provides an antidote. The fact that Cultural Maturity's changes offer a way forward through the complexities and uncertainties ahead may be the most important kind of evidence. I know of no other way of thinking that succeeds at doing so.

Summarizing what Cultural Maturity's changes accomplish appropriately starts with noting what they don't. They don't provide new absolutes or new images of final realization to replace those that are being lost. They also don't offer immediate solutions to today's problems. Much in Cultural Maturity's new picture may be a long time in coming.

But, limitations acknowledged, we've glimpsed how what Cultural Maturity's changes do accomplish could not be more important. We've observed how they make all manner of challenges newly understandable and newly addressable. And we've seen how they make available all the new skills and capacities we've applied in these pages. Of particular significance for this book's reflections, Cultural Maturity's changes also help us get beyond the protective ideological simplifications of times past and bring more encompassing perspective to how we make sense of our worlds. They allow us to engage experience in ways that are more complete and that invite new options. They make it possible to more fully engage and apply the whole of ourselves in all that we do.

There are also Integrative Meta-perspective's more conceptual accomplishments, in particular how it makes possible "post-postmodern" conceptual frameworks such as Creative Systems Theory. We've seen how Creative Systems Theory lets us make kinds of distinctions that become newly important in today's world—with regard to, for example, how cultural systems evolve and how differently the world can look through the eyes of different people. And I've at least touched on how the theory provides a way to address many quite ultimate human questions—as with how it suggests that the truths of science and faith need not ultimately be at odds.[7]

Turning to the question of hope, I find it difficult to be legitimately hopeful about the future if some concept like Cultural Maturity is not basically correct. Here I've put primary emphasis on how getting beyond the polarized and polarizing thinking of times past is necessary to moving forward. But we've also seen how ideological beliefs of any sort ultimately put us at risk.

As far as whether hope is justified, the concept of Cultural Maturity brings both good news and bad news. On the good news side, it suggests that there is in fact a way forward, and one that doesn't depend on utopian solutions. In addition, the recognition that at least the po-

---

[7]   In both *Creative Systems Theory* and my earlier book, *Quick and Dirty Answers to the Biggest of Questions*, I describe multiple other examples where a creative frame helps us address historically perplexing concerns. I will briefly note one more because it relates in important ways to reflections in this book. In a Chapter Five footnote I proposed that a more systemic picture of life has radical implications for how we understand choice in human systems. If we add Creative Systems Theory's more generative understanding of intelligence, we find a provocative polarity-related result—the ability to get beyond the apparent contradiction between the appearance of free will and classical science's deterministic universe, one of philosophy's great quandaries. The short version: Reality as seen through a Modern Age rationalist/mechanistic lens cleanly cleaves human life—where choice is thought of as conscious and free—and the creaturely—where it has been assumed that actions are a product only of mechanistic, reflexive responses. In a related way, it cleaves mind and body. Creative Systems Theory, in better drawing on the whole of intelligence's multiplicity, produces a picture that in each case is more of a whole. When we understand human cognition systemically, will stops being free in the same unfettered sense. Awareness, and with it will, stops being "captain of the cellular ship." We see that while awareness helps facilitate possibility, by itself it doesn't determine it. We also see that this is rather a good thing—indeed, how it is necessary to our strikingly innovative natures. And at the same time, we step beyond thinking of the life of the bodily only in mechanistic/deterministic terms. We find a more dynamic picture all the way around.

tential for Cultural Maturity's changes is developmentally built into who we are makes a strong argument for the conclusions that we may ultimately be up to the task. The fact that we don't have to invent Cultural Maturity's changes from whole cloth is no small thing. There is also a further recognition that at least supports finding the courage needed to engage Cultural Maturity's considerable demands. We've seen how the rewards for doing so could very well be not just exciting, but profound. Cultural Maturity offers more than just a survivable way forward. It invites the possibility of a new depth and completeness in who we are as humans, that we might be not just more intelligent in our choices, but more wise.

The bad news is simply that Cultural Maturity's changes ask a lot of us. I've emphasized how they demand whole new levels of responsibility as well as skills and capacities new to us as a species. And they necessarily involve not just new kinds of ideas, but learning to think in some wholly new ways. Here I've given particular emphasis to how getting beyond Left versus Right ideological thinking stretches us sufficiently that few people as yet are able to do it easily. In suggesting that the greatest factor pushing us beyond what we can tolerate today may be these very changes—the changes that ultimately we must call on if we are to effectively make our way forward—I've also implied that getting there is not guaranteed. Even if the concept of Cultural Maturity is correct, we still can't know for sure whether we can pull off all that its changes ask of us.

I will note one last, particularly provocative implication of Cultural Maturity's cognitive changes. It concerns the concept's long-term significance. I've put primary emphasis in these pages on the concept of Cultural Maturity's importance for today, on what it tells us about the challenges we now face and the capacities required to meet them effectively. But the developmental picture we have looked at supports the conclusion that we can also think of Cultural Maturity's changes as having more extended significance. If what I have outlined is correct,

Cultural Maturity's changes mark not just the beginning of a next chapter in the human story, but the turning of first pages in a new, second kind of story that in the end should define our ultimate human task. It may be that Cultural Maturity's needed "growing up" as a species represents not just the only option for today, it may provide at least general perspective for understanding right thought and action well into humanity's future.

AFTERWORD

Culturally Mature Conversation and
Our Immediate Future

As far as this particular book's task, we are left with two more immediate and concrete questions. First, how in conversations with others do we get beyond polarization and division? I'll offer a few thoughts as far as strategy. I will then return to the question of what the decades immediately ahead will likely require of us.

Supporting Systemic Dialogue

I'm often asked how, if we are committed to culturally mature solutions, do we most usefully interact with people who espouse polarized positions. There is not a simple formula. But there are some good basic principles.[1]

The task necessarily starts by looking closely to see if we are in fact coming from a culturally mature place ourselves. Too often when we

---

[1] You will notice that I have started with a somewhat different question than a person might conventionally ask. The more usual question would be, How do we talk with someone who holds an opposite opinion to our own? There the answer is simple—with basic respect, honesty, and humility. But part of my point with the book is that there are real limits to where even civil debates between opposite positions can go. Real success

feel drawn to engage conversations about divisive topics, we are not. An ideological part in ourselves is wanting to convince an ideological part in the other person. So we have to begin by accepting our own limitations. If we aren't holding the concern from a generally systemic place, it won't matter what we do or say, we will not be effective in our efforts. If we are not confident about where we are coming from, it is best to just keep our mouths shut and get on with doing the needed inner work.

The next step similarly concerns limits, but here the limits are to what it may be possible to accomplish. If a person we are engaging is not at least beginning to address questions in larger ways, we are unlikely to be successful in our efforts, irrespective of our own capacities or how well we communicate. It is essential to be humble to this fact. Trying to convince someone that there is a better way of thinking when they are not ready to hear it will most likely only increase polarization. (If you find yourself struggling with this kind of limit, that is pretty good evidence that you are not in as culturally mature a place as you had assumed.)

If you have gotten this far, the next task is to see if you and the other person can together begin to find a shared objective—or even better, as with this book's inquiry, identify a larger common question. A way to get started is to set aside conclusions about what is true or what should be done and begin to engage more at the level of values. There is a good chance that you and the other person ultimately care about some similar things—such as making the world safe, being sure societies are fair and equitable, affirming the value of life, or having vital economies. Recognizing shared concerns can provide a good starting point for getting to a pertinent more systemic question.

---

requires first finding a culturally mature place in ourselves—which is in fact needed just for the basic respect, honesty, and humility to be real.

For the next step, I will assume that the native inclinations of you and the other person lean in different directions—one of you more to the Right, the other more to the Left.[2] If you and the other person can identify and articulate a shared larger task or question—even just crudely—then take time to examine if assumed conflicting positions are even in limited ways pertinent to addressing it. See if you can understand them as contrasting crayons in the systemic box. Note that here you are not just looking for similarities. The differences are as important, and often more so. You are looking for what you may have been leaving out that the other person can better articulate and bring to the table. Then see if you can begin to bring these differences together in a way that paints a larger picture.

It could also be the case that the native sensibility that you and the other person bring to the conversation are similar—that you have both historically leaned more to the Right or more to the Left in your beliefs. It might seem that then the task would be easier, but in my experience just the opposite is often the case. It can be particularly difficult to recognize the difference between culturally mature views that lean more to the Right or the Left and polarized advocacy that might lean in a similar direction. Indeed, it can be tricky simply to recognize that a distinction needs to be made. But, at least initially, the same basic principles as far as what we need to do hold. The task similarly starts with seeking out and beginning to address a larger question. The only differ-

---

2   It is essential to understand that the fact that a person is capable of culturally mature perspective does not mean that they have equal affinity for the values of the Right and the Left. It only means that they are capable of recognizing that the Right and the Left at their best contribute in important ways to a larger picture. It is quite possible to bring culturally mature perspective to a particular issue and still personally find greatest affinity with sensibilities that ally most with one side of issues or the other. Indeed, that tends most often to be the case. I am most apt to vote Democratic. But I find the common blindnesses of the Left and the Right equally concerning and speak out against both.

ence is that insights in this case will have less to do with appreciating different crayons in the box than with recognizing how the crayon that you together may have preferred by itself fails as an answer. It also involves recognizing how needed larger perspective, while it fundamentally challenges what may have been past shared assumptions, not only better serves general well-being, it is ultimately best for the crayon for which the two of you historically have had greatest affinity.

If you can pull off any of that, it is time to celebrate. Go share a beer.

A Useful Relationship Analogy

A perhaps surprising insight both helps fill out thinking as far as strategy and in another way supports the legitimacy of hope. It also in a further way supports the observation that division itself is the ultimate concern—how it is less that issues divide us, than that polarization itself is dividing us. The insight comes from my work with couples in therapy through the years.

When couples who are experiencing significant discord come to therapy, each person is likely to assume that the solution to their problems lies with the other person changing. Of course this doesn't work. People who are a bit more self-aware may instead conclude that what really needs to happen is for both people to change, which may ultimately be true. But there is an interesting recognition that at first came as a surprise to me. In my experience, it is not the case that both people need to change at the same time or consciously. If one person can learn to love from a more Whole-Person place and stop projecting aspects of themselves onto the other person, that can be enough. And it really doesn't matter which person takes the first step. Once projection from the first person is no longer there to get entangled with, the other person really has no choice but to follow if the two people are to continue to have a relationship.[3]

The most effective strategy for individuals or groups on either the Right or the Left wishing to get beyond the troubling soap opera of political polarization may in similar ways be different from what we might assume. We tend to believe, at least to begin with, that the solution lies with those we disagree with stopping their absurdities. Or, if we are a bit more aware, we might conclude that both sides need to be more aware if we are to make real progress. But in fact the best thing those on either side can do may be to simply get their own house in order. If either the Left or the Right can leave behind past chosen-people/evil-other projections, there may be no need to give attention to needed changes on the part of perceived adversaries. Taking care of changes at home may be what ultimately best supports change all the way around. In another way, we see how the task may be simpler than we think. One strategy pretty much takes care of things. And we don't need to confront the limits of others to pull it off.

There is of course one obvious way the analogy with couples therapy doesn't fully hold. In a personal relationship, if one person can begin to love more from a Whole-Person place and the other can't, either person may simply choose to end things.[4] More collectively we

---

[3]   Further changes, if they occur, often happen in ways that are not obvious. And while they can take time, it is also the case that they can happen more quickly than one might imagine.

[4]   There is in fact another option possible with a relationship that adds a further layer to the analogy. We can choose to be with another person even if there are significant differences in how quickly Whole-Person/Whole-System capacities are acquired. Indeed, culturally mature perspective makes tolerating significant differences more an option. In Chapter Three, I spoke about the extra responsibility that comes with engaging other systems from a culturally mature place when the other system is not yet capable of reciprocating. This observation applies not just to large-scale social systems—the topic in Chapter Three—but also to more personal and local conversations around divisive issues.

really don't have that option. In a quite ultimate sense, we are in it "until death do us part."

Engaging the Years Immediately Before Us

At the end of Chapter One, I suggested that it is quite likely that the next ten to twenty years will be more tumultuous than we might prefer. In the U.S., we thankfully now have national leadership committed to advancement rather than discord.[5] But I've argued that the dynamics that have generated current extreme polarization predated any recent elected leader. There is no reason to think that these factors will go away just because new people are in positions of authority.

I've described how we may well experience at least a short time of greater stability—a period of righting the ship. But we are left with the question of what will happen with the forces of populist Right ethnonationalism that have emerged over the last thirty years once the person who has been their most visible symbol and advocate loses his formal authority. And just as much, we can't yet know what the emerging forces of the neo-socialist populist Left will do once they find that new leadership does not always advocate for their extreme views. Whether we are likely to see a major resurgence of polarization will depend to a significant degree on the answer to the question of how we best understand today's regressive dynamics. It will also depend on our

---

5   How a person responds to this new reality provides a good litmus test for success with the lessons this book has been about, particularly for people on the Left. One could celebrate because basically sane leadership is now a possibility. Or one could celebrate because one's favorite side proved victorious. Given that the emotion is in each case celebration, this might seem an overly subtle distinction. But if our interest is culturally mature possibilities, or even if our interest is simply addressing discord or avoiding a pendulum swing back to the Right with the next election, the distinction has fundamental importance.

ability to recognize the dangers and bring the needed larger perspective to bear.

The potential consequences if we see a major resurgence of polarization are considerable—and arguably simply not an option. We certainly would not benefit from greater social division and inability to communicate. It is also possible that the resulting social unrest in the U.S. could make the country essentially ungovernable. We could easily see widespread dysfunction and chaos playing out around the globe.

I've proposed that the greatest risk concerns how such division distracts us from what I see as the defining task of our time—realizing the kind of "growing up" as a species the concept of Cultural Maturity addresses. We've seen how effectively confronting any of the most important human questions—including multiple questions on which our continued existence may hinge—will require culturally mature understanding. Polar division not only makes new ways of understanding impossible, often it leaves us unable to recognize even that essential new questions exist.

What will the decades immediately ahead require of us specifically with regard to discord and polarization? Certainly, we will need to better recognize the importance of appreciating differences and communicating with basic respect. And at least a bit, they will require that we grasp how differences can reflect complementary truths and begin to think more systemically. Hopefully, here, I've been able to provide a sense of how the task ultimately is to engage a new, more mature developmental chapter in how we understand and act. As I see things, any kind of stability and happiness in the short term—and in the long term our very well-being—depends on our ability to succeed at doing so.

WORDS OF THANKS

The people who have contributed in important ways through the years to the development of Creative Systems Theory are far too numerous to list here. To them I offer a shared thanks. For this particular volume, I wish to express special gratitude to Larry Hobbs, Dan Senour, and Lyn Dillman for their support in the conversations that led to its writing. I also wish to thank Kathy Krause for her skilled editorial work, Teresa Piddington for her editorial assistance, and Wilson Piechazek for his sensitive design of the book's cover.

INDEX

ICD Press is the publishing arm of the Institute for Creative Development. Information about the Institute and other Institute publications can be found on the Institute website at www.CreativeSystems.org or on Charles Johnston's author page at www.CharlesJohnstonmd.com

The Institute for Creative Development (ICD) Press

4324 Meridian Ave. N.
Seattle WA 98103
206-526-8562

ICDPressinfo@gmail.com

Made in the USA
Las Vegas, NV
08 April 2022

47115065R00107